Thanks for
making it
Blessings,

[handwritten signature]

UNCONDITIONAL LOVE: "MOM! DAD! LOVE ME PLEASE!"

By
Sylvia Goldstaub

PUBLISHER

Goldstaub, Delray Beach, Florida

FIRST EDITION

Copyright 1991 Sylvia Goldstaub

Manufactured in the United States of America

ISBN 0-9629414-1-7

ACKNOWLEDGEMENTS

I wish to express my deepest, sincerest thanks to the most loved men in my life—my courageous son, Mark, whose quality of life has guided me through these pages; my dear, devoted, loving, giving son, Paul; and my dear, loving, supportive husband, Bernie.

Mark's spirit will always be with me. Paul was always there for me. Bernie has been my pillar of strength and never-ending love. I also acknowledge with gratitude and respect Mark's devoted, loving, long-time companion, Edmund Wojcik, who gave so much happiness, love and respect to all of us.

Thanks to Cousin Steve Schwartz of Los Angeles, California, for giving of himself at every request. Thanks to Marks's wonderful friends, who were constantly at his side, and who encouraged him to *keep up the battle*. I also thank Debbie Openden, who knew Mark longer than anyone else outside his immediate family. She and he shared a special love and respect for one another. The beautiful Memorial Quilt she made for him will forever be inscribed in my mind. And I acknowledge Cathy Blaivas, Marilyn Briskin, Mark Jollie, Dan Kellachan and Virginia Gillick, members of the Mark Goldstaub Public Relations Team.

Special thanks to Pauline Perez, Marks's *adopted grandmother*; Shelly Gross of Westbury Music Fair, whose friendship, caring compassion, understanding, and support encouraged me to complete this book; Lisa Feldman, M.S.M., with the Jewish Family Service of South Palm Beach County Jewish Federation, whose counseling helped me through my emotional, physical and psychological crisis; Anita Rosenkrantz, teacher, lecturer and writer, whose inspiration guided me through many rough spots; my sister, Helen Colton, in Los Angeles, for her reassurance and constructive suggestions toward my goal; my sister Rae Rosenberg, in Florida, who was there when I needed her; my brother Ben Grossman, sister-in-law Myra Grossman, in Florida; Bernie's sister and brother-in-law; Estelle and Mac Goldstein in Miami Beach, for their moral support; all my nieces, nephews and relatives around the country; Cousin Dorothy Cole, in Florida; my closest cousin from childhood, Melvin Kessler, and his friend Vic Bala; my friends and neighbors who stood behind us (you know who you are) Jim Sugarman of the Comprehensive AIDS Program (CAP); Paulette

Goodman, president of Parents and Friends of Lesbians and
Gays (P-FLAG); Camille Bartczak and Leonard Dean (members of P-FLAG) in Culver City, California, who arranged for
radio and TV interviews for my book and who went out of their
way after a busy workday to drive me around Los Angeles and
adjacent towns for interviews for this book.
What can I say about GOD'S LOVE WE DELIVER, INC.?
Well, *THANKS!* is not enough. These fine people deliver hot,
nutritious meals to homebound people who have AIDS. They
do it daily, and free of charge. GOD'S LOVE WE DELIVER
gave Mark much peace of mind. I will forever be grateful.
Thanks also to the library research staff; Anthony Verdesca Jr.;
Bob Davidson of the West Atlantic branch, Delray Beach,
Florida; Loretta Pompilio in Trumansburg, New York (The
Phoenix Book Store); my editor, Leslie Puryear, in
Trumansburg, New York, for her guidance, patience and com-
passion; Tom Danciu, founder of the Legacy Foundation (thank
you for including my poem, "*Ode To My Son, Mark*" on the jacket
of your *Legacy* album; Steve Biller of the Sun Sentinel and his
editor, Vicki Preuss; Fran Hathaway of the Palm Beach Post;
Bobby LaFont and Sheldon Katz, with Long Beach California
Cable TV; Terry Villaire, of the Boca Raton AIDS Support
Group, for his personal support; and Dr. Mervyn Silverman,
president of the American Foundation for AIDS Research
(AMFAR); and Dr. Martin Kleiman.
Also, special thanks to those who have given me permission to
write about their lives, and to Ron Hymowitz, Delray Beach
Post Office, for helping me with mailings and to Irv Gale.
My deepest thanks and gratitude also to my publisher, Harbor
City Publications in Melbourne, Florida—Coleen Moore and
her husband, David, for their insight, guidance and direction,
and to John Waters for editing and typesetting.
    If I have omitted anyone, please forgive me.

***Without All You Caring, Humane, Beings
I May Not Have Been Able To Write This Book.***

Sylvia Goldstaub

PREFACE

Do we know we don't know? Do we know we don't know if we have the choice to select the course of our lives?

Do we know we can turn the *Stream of Destiny* which sets our lives in motion? Do we know we don't know what makes a *HUMANE* being?

Do we know we don't know what makes a person *heterosexual, homosexual* or *lesbian?*

This book is about a fine *HUMANE BEING*, my son, Mark. A kind, tender, merciful, considerate, compassionate homosexual, he died of AIDS on December 14, 1988. This is a story of his courageous two-year battle for *survival*. Determined to live, he faced the odds and never gave up *hope*. He used the powers of his mind to pull himself through many crises.

These are the humanistic words of his life's greatest struggle—the relationships, love, compassion, understanding, and acceptance among Mark, as an AIDS patient; and his parents, brother, and close companion, Edmund Wojcik. It is also a story of Mark's feelings, thoughts, actions and reactions, all of which were intertwined with his family and friends. He *knew* we loved him, respected him, admired him, and that we were and always will be very proud of him.

Unlike Mark's loving parents, estranged parents are literally destroying their own flesh and blood by not accepting their own sons or daughters.

I sincerely hope that this book, written from my heart and mind, will help re-establish *family ties* for the good health and peace of mind of all other sincere, loving human beings. Human societies need to know and accept the *humanistic side of AIDS* and realize that now is the time to mend fences and meet with each other on good terms.

If this book reaches the heart of just one family, my son, Mark Goldstaub, has not died in vain, and his relatively short life on Earth has served humankind.

If we do not listen, let adversity teach us.

Sylvia Goldstaub

FOREWORD

Sylvia Goldstaub made a deep impression on me when she first enrolled in my class, "*Mind, Matter and Meditation.*" A charming woman, petite and well groomed, she was an alert and attentive student, eager to learn. Her mind was sharp, keen and inquisitive.

Then one day she made a startling statement in class. In a quiet and controlled voice she said, "I lost my son, Mark, two years ago. He was thirty-seven years old, and he died from AIDS."

I was stunned! What an amazing woman to be able to make this painful announcement to a group of strangers!

Everyone in the class was given the assignment to introduce himself or herself in a few words. Sylvia did not have to reveal herself in this manner, but she did. I admired her courage and honesty.

A close friendship developed between Sylvia and me. I was able to witness her growth as she worked on this book, which was dedicated to her son, Mark. It was with great awareness of the profound emotional turmoil of her being that Sylvia pressed onward to produce this noble literary work. I feel proud to have been able, in a small way, to have provided some editorial assistance in her endeavor.

This book is a labor of love. Sylvia depicts the heroic struggle of her son to survive and overcome this devastating disease.

He lost the battle, but he won the love and respect of all who knew him for the beautiful, courageous and caring person he was. his parents and brother were with him to share the valiant struggle and his final days of life. They were always there for him — in love and in sorrow. This book proves there can be victory after death.

One day this disease will be conquered, but until then, AIDS patients require the *unconditional love* and support of their parents, families and friends. Their suffering is beyond ordinary comprehension. But to be abandoned by their parents and families is the cruelest thrust of all.

Give them your unconditional love and devotion, especially in the last stages of their illness. This is Sylvia's message to the world.

Anita Rosenkrantz
Teacher, Writer, Lecturer

Anita Rosenkrantz and Sylvia Goldstaub

CONTENTS

*How does a parent come to terms with
the death of a son, a brilliant young press agent
for the theater, at the age of thirty-seven?*

*In a mere 37 years, Mark Goldstaub
became famous in his career. The New York
Times publishes obituaries only for
those who have achieved prominance.*

*This Book Is Dedicated
To The Memory of Our Beloved
Son and Brother
Mark Neil Goldstaub
With Love From Mom, Dad and Brother Paul*

THE THREE FATES
In Greek or Roman Mythology . . .

The Three Goddesses Who Control Human
Destiny and Life:

The First, Clotho, Spins the Thread of Life.
The Second, Lachesis, Determines the Length.
The Third, Atropos, Cuts it Off!

There is just so much thread on the Spool of Life!

I. This Legacy I Leave My Loved Ones:

The meaning of *Unconditional Love* from my family and friends. Thank you so very much for bearing with me these so very unhappy days.

The support, friendship and love I've felt from you, my family and friends, helps me fight on. I'm lucky and enriched by everyone I touch and love who, in turn, love me. You will always be in my heart. The love, support, compassion, caring and acceptance from all of you is almost more than I can endure.

Edmund, my loving companion, you are always at my side. You give me so very much happiness. I'll always remember the wonderful happy times we share. I'll miss you terribly. Be happy. I love you.

To my brother, Paul, you are always here for me. The squabbles we had while growing up were just sibling rivalry. I'm proud of you. You have great talent. Your music has been an inspiration to me and will remain in my heart. Be happy. I'll miss you. I love you.

To my many friends, Debbie, Cathy, Virginia, Dan, Mark Jollie, and others who make me feel I am their family, I thank you for being there for me in every aspect of my life.

To my loving parents . . . What can I say to ease your pain? You've been remarkable with your devotion and respect for me at every turn, with *Your Unconditional Love*, your acceptance, your compassion, your inner knowing and acknowledging my every need. I know you are suffering, but not allowing this suffering to overtake us when you visit with me during all the painful times helps me more than I can ever say. My one wish is that you will be able to carry on your lives as you taught me. I know your lives will never be the same. Try to be happy—keep on dancing, no matter how hard it gets. I'll always be with you, in spirit, in my soul, and through all eternity. I love you both so very much. I'll miss you. Until we meet again,

Mark
Spring 1988

MARK GOLDSTAUB, 37
PRESS AGENT IN THE ARTS

Mark Goldstaub, a press agent for many performing-arts organizations, died of acquired immune deficiency syndrome yesterday at his home in Manhattan. He was 37 years old.

Mr. Goldstaub was president of Mark Goldstaub Public Relations, a New York concern that he founded in 1982. His clients included the Metropolitan Opera House, the Paris Opera Ballet, the National Ballet of Canada and the Westbury Music Fair on Long Island. He also publicized tributes to such performers as Shirley MacLaine, Mary Martin, Katherine Hepburn, Hume Cronym and Jessica Tandy. Before starting his own company, Mr. Goldstaub worked for Ballantine Books and agencies that represented various Broadway shows. His long-time companion was Edmund Wojcik.

Mr. Goldstaub is survived by his parents, Bernard and Sylvia Goldstaub of Delray Beach, Fla. and a brother, Paul, of Ithaca, N.Y.

CHAPTER ONE

The "Champ" Was Our Son

I searched for answers. At moments such as this, now more than ever, my faith was challenged.

My parents had a casual attitude toward religion. As I matured, married and had children, I don't think a day went by that, after a crisis of some sort, I didn't look to the sky and say, "*Thank you, God!*"

But with the passing of years I couldn't help but question, "Is someone up there?"—supposedly running the show. Why does He allow such horrible events to take place, such as the Holocaust, wars, drugs, famine, muggings, illnesses which cannot be cured, and innocent young people and old people being killed senselessly? I can continue endlessly naming these nightmares. Now, the plague AIDS! Why are the young, vibrant, productive, talented, fine males and females being taken from us in the prime of their lives? They are our bright, brilliant future leaders of the world.

I lack the courage today to look to the sky and say, "It is a fraud, no one is there." I can best describe myself as an unknowing agnostic. It is impossible now for me to know whether there is a God or future life or anything beyond material phenomena.

We know that we don't know! But we must be factual or realistic, and realize that today is Thursday, yesterday was Wednesday and tomorrow will be Friday.

This is a fact. Mark, our dearly loved son, conceived with love, was a gift given to us for such a short time. Now he is gone from us forever. We were told by well-wishers, sympathizers, "Remember the good times, the happy days you all shared."

My husband and Mark's father, Bernie, remembered "the good times past" as his crutch. However, my mental handicap was asking, "Why couldn't the 'good and happy' times continue? Is the glass half-full or half-empty?"

On Wednesday, December 7, 1988, at about 2:30 in the afternoon, after visiting some few days with Mark in New York, Bernie and I left him with love, hugs and kisses. We then caught an airline flight back to Florida. We had followed that routine many times during the previous year and a half. Encouraged by his buoyant attitude and high spirits, we were wrapped in the euphoria of high hope and optimism.

Mark had spent most of the morning on the telephone, conducting business between his office and home. He had just made arrangements for theater tickets to the matinee performance of a new Broadway show for the following Wednesday, December 14th. He intended to take his nurse, Pauline, a warm, loving compassionate human being—and his "adopted Grandma"—to the theater for the show.

It was instant love between Pauline and Mark! I am so grateful for Pauline. She protected and watched over him like a mother hen. She did not permit visitors with colds, nor did she allow visitors to touch him. Everyone understands and respects her. Pauline was such a great comfort to Mark during his last days. At night, Edmund gave him the company and comfort he sorely needed.

I was in the bedroom with Mark when he finalized the theater arrangements. Pauline was in the kitchen. He called out, "Pauline, wear your best bib and tucker! We two are going to see a new Broadway show next Wednesday at matinee. December 14th! Mark your calendar."

Pauline yelled back, "Okay Mark, we have a date!" She came into the bedroom and continued, "Young man, have you forgotten I am a married woman?" Their contagious sense of humor rose to the occasion. We all laughed. I especially enjoyed the deep hearty laugh, coming from my son.

When I spoke with him by telephone on Saturday, December 10th, he felt he might be coming down with a cold.

"But Mom, I'll overcome this just as I have the other times. Remember, I'm *The Champ*!" During the previous many months, I had called him The Champ for his winning out over his many trials. He was so proud of that title.

"Okay Champ," I answered. "I'll speak with you in a few days."

Right-O, love you both," he told me. "Bye!"

"We love you too," I said. "Take care. Bye!"

I had no way of knowing that was the last time I would ever speak to my son, Mark, again.

On Tuesday night, December 13th, about 8:30, I was about to call him from Florida when my telephone rang. It was Edmund, Mark's long-time companion and dear friend. Mark had taken a turn for the worse, Edmund explained. Mark was having difficulty breathing and his doctor had just brought over a large hospital-size oxygen tank.

I wanted to fly to New York immediately, but the doctor got on the phone to reassure me.

"Sylvia," he said, "Mark's determination and remarkable recovery power have pulled him through many crises. It is not as bad as I thought. He will be here for the holidays and into next Easter holidays as well."

Edmund relayed Mark's message: *to wait another day.*

At 6:25 Wednesday morning, December 14, 1988, my phone rang again and, as it did, I knew my son Mark was gone from me forever.

"Sylvia, this is Pauline," she said sadly. "Please take a deep breath, keep breathing slowly and deeply. I'm so sorry to have to tell you we just *lost* Mark. He left us just a few minutes ago, peacefully, without pain, as was his wish. He was ready, with dignity and grace . . ."

My Champ was gone. I'll never again hear him say, "Love you both! Bye."

I can't say I remember much after that for a while. Bernie was on an extension phone, and we were both drowning in tears as I spoke next to Edmund. Like robots, their buttons being pushed, Bernie and I called our other son, Paul. The three of us were incoherent. I next called my sister, who also lives in Florida, then for airline reservations.

I called Edmund back, wanting to know *what, how, when* and *why*? I told him our flight plan and that we would make all burial arrangements. Edmund informed me that everything had "already been taken care of. Mark left full instructions." Edmund then said he would give us details when we arrived in New York.

"Don't let anybody touch him," I pleaded. "I want to see the way he left us."

I didn't remember any of those conversations until days later. In times of stress, we often find we have strengths we didn't know existed.

I somehow managed to pack. As I reached into my closet for something black, the one thought racing through my mind was that *parents are not supposed to outlive their children.* There I was, packing something black to wear to the funeral of my wonderful 37-year-old son, who once had his whole life ahead of him. Where was the justice in this miserable world?

As I stood, holding a black outfit, my mind wandered back to the many times he said to me, "Gee mom, you look so great in bright colors. I love to see you in green, red, orange or yellow. Don't you ever wear dark shades?"

Needless to say, his never-ending compliments and approval of my choice of colors and style of clothes were a thorough joy.

"Mark, I love wearing bright colors," I would tell him. "For me, they are symbols of happiness."

I was so very tempted to wear a bright-colored outfit, because I knew he would have loved it. It would have been a shared moment for the last time, but would society understand my being so untraditional? I wondered. Should I please society and follow tradition, above my tragic personal feelings, by wearing black?

Can a mother possibly describe the torture of packing, getting to the airport, waiting there for her flight, under these circumstances? How does she survive those horrible hours until she reaches the side of a dear son who had passed away just hours before?

Other people were going about their daily routines, not knowing I had lost my child. I wondered how they could so casually go their own merry ways.

Edmund and his sister, Rita, met us at the airport. They were waiting to take us to the funeral parlor.

"No! No! I want to see Mark first," I insisted.

Edmund explained that Mark was at the funeral parlor, not at the apartment. By law, they had to remove the body as soon as possible. He assured me he had spoken to the proper parties at the Chapel and they were not touching Mark until we saw him. In fact, they were waiting for us, no matter what time we got there. It was too late, however, for Mark's brother to see him. Paul could not get a flight from Ithaca until later in the afternoon.

Bernie and I had our private moments with our dearly loved son. He was lying on a flat surface, a blanket covering his body to the neck. He looked so much at rest, and so peaceful. His terrible ordeal of two and a half years was finally over.

I stroked his hair, kissed him on the forehead, kissed his cheeks, kissed him on the lips. As his mustache touched my lips, I vividly recalled the time he graduated from college.

He had a rather long beard and a mustache protruded over his lips. After being home for about a week or so for rest and relaxation, he came to the conclusion it was time to get out into the world and make a name for himself. He came down to breakfast one morning completely clean shaven, dressed with shirt and tie.

"Mom, I'm ready to find my way. I'm going into New York to find a job!"

I said, "Mark, you look great without all that hair all over your face. Dad and I are so proud of you. But, I think you'd better grow back the mustache. It will make you look older.

After a few weeks, he did grow back the mustache and never again shaved it off.

With tears running down my cheeks, I kissed him again and again on the lips. I ran my fingers through his hair once more. I traced my fingers over his forehead, down his nose, across his cheeks, and gently placed my right hand on his lips, making an indelible impression of his face upon my fingers forever.

As I was removing my hand from his face, my bracelet he had given me for my birthday caught in the blanket near his chin. I could not unravel the blanket thread from the bracelet. I had to tear the thread to get loose.

A very strange feeling overcame me. My son enjoyed my fingers massaging his face, catching his blanket on my bracelet!

I imagined him telling me to keep massaging his face, for it felt good. I wondered if he was telling me not to leave yet, but to stay longer.

He had always enjoyed my giving him a back massage in the morning, after I awakened him for school, and many times when we were together.

"Mom," he would say, "What a great way to start the day. A massage is so stimulating and good for circulation."

I again kissed his lips. My fingers moved over his face again, slowly, with a massaging touch. I bent down and held him tightly with Bernie's arms around us. We stayed as long as we could.

As we turned to leave, we cried, "We love you, son, and always will. Somewhere, someplace, somehow, we will be together again. Have peace. We miss you."

In the car, on the way to the apartment, Edmund told us of the instructions Mark had left for him.

Our son's love for us could not have been more apparent. Even in his death, he protected his mother, father and brother from having to go through the horrible experiences of making burial arrangements for a young son and brother while in the stages of deep grief.

Mark wanted a specifically shaped, natural pine-finish casket with a Star of David on the top. His wish was to be cremated and to have his remains scattered over the waters of the coast of Maine. Mark and Edmund shared their love of nature's beauty. They both felt this area was one of the most beautiful spots they had ever visited.

Edmund placed the most recent photo of Mark on top of the closed casket. He wanted people to remember Mark as he was in life. We will be forever grateful to Edmund, our son's partner in marriage, for his kindness.

The very Wednesday Mark would have been so thrilled about taking his nurse, Pauline, to a new Broadway show turned out to be the day he died.

To the end, his success as press agent in the arts prevailed. Mark would have been very proud. As the saying goes in theater, *he drew a sell-out!*

In due time, the Chapel filled to capacity. Friends of the past, friends of the present, aunts, uncles, cousins, his working family, colleagues and clients came. I was told people were standing on the stairs all the way out to the sidewalk. Hundreds came from all over to pay their respect to our fine young son who had loved everyone UNCONDITIONALLY. And they returned his unconditional love.

During the course of the year since our son left us and my decision to write this book, Mark's friends have been a source of strength for me. We maintain a fine rapport, and I am deeply grateful.

The four dearest people who were the closest to him over many years gave the eulogies at the services.

CHAPTER TWO

Eulogies for Mark Goldstaub

Friday, December 16, 1988

Deborah Openden

Mark's Dear, Long-Time Close Friend.

Dan Kellachan

Mark's First Employee.

Mark Jollie

He Is Saint Mark Jollie; Always There For You.

Edmund Wojcik

Mark's Friend, Companion, Lover and Marriage Partner.

Deborah's Eulogy

It turned out that the most difficult part of preparing this was trying to figure out how to begin—but that was accomplished. I would next like to thank Edmund for asking me to speak today.

Although the past two years have been very difficult, what comes to mind when I think of Mark is lots of love and a smile for all of the wonderful times we shared together.

I met Mark 16 years ago in Boston. He called me up one night and introduced himself as I was having a migraine. He talked so fast and my head hurt so much that I just agreed to whatever he said which, in that instance, was to meet each other Saturday night!. When we did meet, it definitely was *love at first sight.*

I can't think of much that Mark and I haven't shared over the years. There are many stories and, frankly, a lot of them are downright silly. But what I would like to share with you today is something which I think exhibits Mark's indomitable *spirit.* I came up to visit Mark during his last hospitalization.

He was very frail, in a lot of discomfort, and he had just had a procedure done. I had brought some music along that I thought he might enjoy. When Bobby McFerrin sang, *"Don't Worry, Be Happy,"* Mark got out of bed and danced with me. That was Mark. During this long ordeal, Mark maintained his positivity and his love of life. He worked hard and he always had a word of love for me—no matter how badly he felt.

I feel we have reason to be grateful this day. Grateful to have known and loved such a special person who touched us all. Grateful for the love, friendship, laughter, generosity and caring which Mark showed to all his loved ones. And grateful for the peace and rest he so deserved and which are his now.

I want to acknowledge my dear, sweet friend, Edmund, for being Mark's true life support system and also to say that from the moment I met Edmund, I knew Mark had found his soul's partner. Their relationship was, and always will be, a source of inspiration and hope for me.

I would also like to acknowledge Mark's parents, Sylvia and Bernie, who have lovingly stood by Mark and Edmund

11

throughout this most difficult trial. We also share our prayers with Mark's brother, Paul. If we learn nothing else from all of this, other than the limitless power of love, then I believe we have learned well.

I would like to read a very brief passage from a book called *Many Wonderful Things*. The information quoted is from the other side, from another plane:

> The question asked is, "What would be the sensation and the effect when the soul leaves the body and goes into the resting place?"
>
> And the reply is, "It is a great release, a great freedom, a release from bondage—a recognition that death is not an ending, nor a beginning, but a returning to a joyous time—a time of peace, a time of rest, of understanding—a great spiritual union with things known before. For the house, the temple, fades away and disappears for a shining new temple each time that we return. There is nothing to fear, nothing to abhor; but rather, a great, joyous, wonderful returning to where you have been many times before.

I am sure you will all join me in wishing Mark *shalom*, goodbye, hello and peace always, forever.

Deborah Openden

Dan's Eulogy

Six years ago Mark Goldstaub interviewed me for a position in his newly formed company. He was about to open for business and I was excited by the "glamorous" prospect of working for a *real press agent*. Mark took a chance and hired me after warning me about "life in the theater." At that time, he showed me a quote attributed to the legendary press agent, Richard Maney, on a yellowing slip of paper, which Mark received when he had decided to become a Broadway press agent. The quote was this:

"Press agentry is no business for people with nerve. But it can be a good life for one with detachment, sympathy for the deranged, and an understanding of why the theater's children behave the way they do."

Mark kept that slip of paper pinned to his bulletin board; and I now have passed it along to all of you, perhaps as an insight to a very complex man whose love and understanding for those who surrounded him was matched only by his determination to succeed in his chosen field. Mark was, at times, intense and volatile, but it was his warm heart and his affection that made him most successful.

In 1982, when I started to work for Mark, he landed his first client, the San Francisco Symphony Orchestra. Shortly thereafter, we were hired by the Westbury Music Fair Group to represent the Westbury Music Fair. As each new year approached, Mark would invariably add a new client, which would excite him and promise new growth for his business, which was growing more and more successful. There were Broadway shows, concerts, tributes, national tours, and the Metropolitan Opera.

To say the least, we were very busy. In 1984, while representing the "*On Broadway Concert Series*" at the Gershwin Theater, Mark presented Shirley MacLaine with an elephant he had borrowed from the Ringling Brothers and Barnum and Bailey Circus—for her 50th birthday, fulfilling one of her fantasies. It was one of Mark's proudest achievements and the event was later chronicled in Shirley MacLaine's memoir, *"Dancing in the Light."*

Mark taught me that, to be a successful press agent, I must be a diplomat, gifted writer, tactfully persistent "idea man," talented communicator (with the "gift of gab"), a resourceful individualist, dedicated craftsman, and compassionate hand-holder. Perhaps most importantly, he taught me the necessity of maintaining a sense of humor and to be secure enough to place the demands of my ego after those of everybody else.

Mark Goldstaub left me an invaluable legacy. As an apprentice, I learned the trade of press agentry. With him, I saw the ups and downs of life in the theater and the comings and goings of clients. In the office, when the work was overbearing and next to impossible, we would all turn to each other and say, "Now, this is glamorous!"

Under his wing, I became a senior press agent, and I am proud of his many public and private successes. Facing the future without being able to turn around and ask him, *"What's next?"* fills me with trepidation. I only hope to continue to live up to his exceedingly high standards and to continue to make him proud.

Mark loved life and made everyone near him part of his extended family. Each of us benefitted in some way from knowing and loving him, and I suspect he drew upon us all for love and support throughout his life, especially during his fight with AIDS.

In one of our last conversations, I thanked Mark for his courage and told him that he was *an inspiration to me.* Each year, at this time, there was something to celebrate at Mark Goldstaub Public Relations, and it would be on to bigger and better things. I can't help believing that this year is no exception; for surely, Mark Goldstaub, an extraordinary man, is now at work on bigger and better things than this life could offer.

Thank you.

Dan Kellachan

Mark Jollie's Eulogy

Mark faced his illness and, ultimately, his death with the same senses of curiosity and commitment with which he lived the rest of his life. Certainly, Mark would not have consciously chosen his battle with AIDS, nor the need to face death at such a young age. However, as Mark realized that these possibilities were in his future, he set out to learn as much as possible and as quickly—yet thoroughly—as possible.

No relevant area was left unexplored. From minute medical details, political realities and their ramifications, social and psychological considerations, to personalities of researchers and health care providers, and much more, Mark's thirst for information was constant. In his educational, professional, and interpersonal lives, Mark had not been one to leave any stone unturned—and he was certainly not about to allow that while his life was, literally, at stake.

Time spent visiting Mark as his illness progressed was always characterized by insightful questioning. And when Mark asked a question, he listened carefully and discerningly to the answer. He seemed to feel his major (if not his only) defense against this terrible disease was knowledge. I suspect he was right.

Mark, a truly compassionate and loving person that I have been privileged to know, refused to let the details of his own illness blot out his concern for the welfare of others. No matter how severe Mark's situation at the time, we never had a visit or conversation end without spending time discussing Edmund's welfare, the lives of Mark's family, his friends, the conditions of other clients, and my health and emotional stability (or lack thereof). It is always a profound experience when I observe the constancy of *true compassion.*

Throughout the course of Mark's illness, he managed to keep his mind infused with thoughts of healing, wellness and involvement with life to the fullest. There were many times when none of us could figure out how he accomplished this, but neither could we deny he was doing it. There came a time, however, when it was clear to Mark that the time of his passing was growing near and that he needed to devote some energy to making his death as characteristically "*Goldstaub*" as every minute of his life had been.

My last conversation with Mark on Sunday, December 11, 1988, just a few days before he died, was spent dealing—in the most realistic terms—with death, fears and possibilities. Mark was hungrier than ever for information which I have gleaned from my work with other friends and clients who were also facing death, as well as my interpretation of my recent research into various spiritual disciplines. Mark, ever the scientist, ever the student, was determined to tackle death with every obtainable shred of information.

The courage with which Mark entered into the final phase, which encompassed his willingness to experience doubt and fear, was most *impressive*. At a time when Mark was already encountering extreme loss of physical strength, severe visual limitations, and no small amount of pain, he delved into his fears about the process of dying itself, and the possibilities of the *unknown state* following death. In truth, none of us know how we will react should we be given an extended period of time to contemplate our death and potential life thereafter. I do know, however, that should I find myself in that situation, my experience will certainly be colored by memories of the strength of character and personal courage which Mark Goldstaub displayed throughout our last moments together.

I will be eternally grateful for the lessons which Mark, both actively and passively, taught me —*through his strength, humor and commitment to life and compassion*. I have no doubt that seeds which he planted in my life—and in the lives of so many others—will continue to bear loving fruit for a long time, and through the many, varied challenges which we will encounter. Mark was an amazing *MAN*.

I Miss You Mark!

Mark Jollie

Edmund's Eulogy

Thank you all for coming. Mark would have been very pleased to have a *sold-out house: standing room only*. I want to thank you for all the support, love and friendship you gave us in his hours of need in the last years. Someone once defined a true friend as a person who comes in the door when the world is rushing out. And many of you certainly qualify in that category.

And to Mark I say, I wish we didn't have to say *goodbye*. There were still so many things to do together, so many thoughts to share and so many memories to recall. So, let's not say goodbye. Let's just make the best of our new situation; because as long as there are memories, and thoughts, we won't really be apart.

Mark didn't like to talk about the reality that we must all face: *our own death*. After he was diagnosed with AIDS, it took him over a year and a half to write his will. Information about his final wishes came in dribs and drabs, here and there.

When we were driving to the country one weekend, listening to the score from the Broadway musical "*Les Miserables*", a song was playing called "*Bring Him Home.*" I turned to Mark, who was also crying, and he said, "I want this played at my memorial." And, so we will now end the service by playing the song he asked for . . .

Edmund Wojcik

Paul, Bernie, Mark and Sylvia Goldstaub

CHAPTER THREE

Tomorrow Will Be Better

On the flight back to Florida, I sat beside Bernie, gazing through the airplane window. The sky was clear and blue, with white, puffy clouds scattered below. I visualized *my son Mark* in the far distance. I could see him coming closer and closer, a contagious smile on his face.

I could hear his familiar voice saying, "Hi Mom! Hi Dad! Don't worry! Be happy! I'll always be with you! I love you both!" He did not say "*Bye.*"

For the rest of our flight, I relived the eighteen months since he had first told us he had AIDS. Bernie and I had just returned North from spending the winter in Florida. We had looked forward to spending summers at our apartment in New Jersey, where we often visited with our children, *Paul, Mark* and *Edmund*.

We often met them in Manhattan for dinner, and to enjoy seeing such things as the newest Broadway shows, ballets or operas at the Met. The fascination of Broadway has always mesmerized me. Sometimes we went to Shea Stadium and enjoyed a baseball game—our team being the Mets.

Paul, our son and Mark's brother, often joined us for long weekends at Mark's mountain house—a get-away from the hustle and bustle of New York City. The house, a Cape Cod, was painted black and white and set upon a small hill which overlooks a lovely, natural lake.

The five of us enjoyed long walks there, appreciating the joys of Mother Nature. In the evenings, we would sit out on the patio—which overlooks the lake. On clear nights, the stars seemed so very close that we felt we could reach out and grab them.

Strains of Paul's beautiful music would often be playing in the background. He is a composer and Professor of Music at Ithaca College in upstate New york. Sharing such quality time with my family has always been pure *ecstasy*. These are qualities which make life worth living.

My birthday is in January. Edmund was born in December, Mark in April, Bernie in May, and Paul in July. For years, Bernie and I have celebrated our wedding anniversary in June, when we can all be together as family. Traditionally, this has been *One Big Shindig!*. We always had a ball! Those were grand and glorious times in our lives.

On one Friday night in late June 1987, two weeks after one of our great parties, my world *EXPLODED!* It began after Mark and Edmund had driven from New York City to our place in New Jersey to join us for dinner at home.

Just as we finished with coffee and dessert, and as I was about to suggest we sit out on the terrace and enjoy the evening's coolness, Mark asked, "Mom, could I please have another cup of coffee? And would you please sit down. I need to tell you and Dad something that is *very important*."

Expecting cheerful news, I served him coffee, smiled, sat down and said, "O.K. son! I'm all ears! Tell me the news!"

I jokingly placed my hands behind my ears, and pushed them forward to *hear his message.* I expected him to laugh, but his face was gray with seriousness.

As I sat and looked at him, I realized his mood was *very serious.*

It must have been my motherly instinct which caused me to ask, "*What's wrong, son?*" We were both sitting down, facing each other, and Bernie was listening attentively.

Mark, with his lovely, bearded face and beautiful eyes, looked into our faces, and began to explain.

"Mom, Dad, I love you both. I wish with all my heart I could spare you this, but the time has come for me to tell you. I don't know any other way than to just be honest and tell you the *truth*."

Edmund was with us, and as Mark paused, looked across the table and, stared into my eyes, he hesitated for a moment. Then, he shared his heart, mind, soul and body. Like the man he always was, he firmed up his voice and told us, "*I have AIDS.*"

The shock of his valiant, shared communication with those he loved most was—to us who were there—like that of a stabbing knife.

Mark continued, "My doctor has *diagnosed* me, and said that if this has to be, it is much better now than it would have been five years ago. The doctor explained that *we have more knowledge than ever before about AIDS. More research is now being done and chances for survival are better now. The medical profession does not yet have a cure, but we do have medications which help keep the disease under control.*"

Mark continued to talk as I flooded him with questions. I was hearing his voice, but my mind was in such a *whirl* I could not grasp the meaning of his words.

Inside, I was churning. My consciousness and sanity seemed to be losing control. I do remember, however, that as I stared at my wonderful, beautiful Mark, I had the awful feeling that I was seeing him for *the last time*.

I still can visualize his natural brown hair, alert dark brown eyes, the slight bump on his nose, (which he always hated), his well maintained mustache, the texture of his skin, his contagious smile, lovely white teeth, and strong athletic body. I felt as if I were absorbing every living fiber of his being.

Suddenly, tears burst and I began to shake. He came to my side, held me, hugged me and shared with his tears.

21

Edmund walked Bernie into the bedroom to assist him with handling the enormous shock and surprise of what Mark had just said.

Mark and I embraced for a while, both breathing deeply, then I found control. We then joined Bernie and Edmund.

The four of us sat intimately as time ticked away, and Mark's always present optimism managed to override our depression and instill a hopeful attitude.

We dealt with our feelings a while; Mark and Edmund prepared to leave. We walked them to their car, parted with love, kisses, hugs and high *hopes*. Bernie and I watched them drive away.

When the two of us were alone, Bernie looked toward the starlighted sky and cried out, "Take me! Please! Leave my son well and happy. Oh, Lord, he has his whole life ahead of him, and I've been hanging around a long time. It's not fair."

We put our arms around each other and weakly walked back inside the apartment.

As we lay in bed that night, trying to sort things out before sleeping, I could hear Mark's words still ringing in my ears, "I have AIDS! I have AIDS! I have AIDS!"

I remembered some of the other things he told us, while we listened as best as we could.

"I'm doing fine now . . . medication helping . . . Power of Mind . . . New Coming of Age Healing Method . . . *Creative Visualization* . . . Proper Nutrition! . . . Exercise! . . . I'll make it!—all five-foot-ten of me.

"I come from good stock . . . mind is powerful . . . full of intelligence . . . I can visualize and create my own wellness . . . Eat, sleep and breathe *wellness* . . . Creative Visualization! . . .

Mark's litany of reassurance was endless; but in my grief, I wondered if I actually heard him say those words or if it was all a bad dream.

Mark had first been diagnosed with AIDS in July 1986. His doctor subsequently prescribed AZT, the only approved medication for AIDS, at that time, in the United States.

At the time of Mark's revelation, he was doing well on that medication, and he felt he had no urgent need to tell us about his illness. He thought, "Why make my parents worry needlessly?" I am sure he also hoped and prayed the time would never come for him to need to tell us.

Looking back, I recall when he visited us in Florida in December 1986. During his stay, I remember he often sat on the terrace, overlooking the lake, and remarked how water makes one feel so calm, peaceful and serene.

I remember one day, when a breeze was slowly blowing through the palm trees, heated by a warm sun, and illuminated by a blue sky. The view was soothing, calming, tranquil and peaceful.

I was preparing dinner that late afternoon. As I looked out the pass-through from the kitchen onto the terrace, I saw Mark sitting so still, not moving. I watched a short time, then walked out and asked, "Mark, Dear, are you feeling okay? I was watching you from the kitchen, and you were *so still*."

As I spoke, I noticed he was holding a book, *Creative Visualization,* by Shakti Gawain, which he had been reading.

He answered, "Mom, I'm okay. I was meditating. This is the perfect setting for it!"

I apologized for disturbing him then asked about the book. "The title sounds interesting," I said. "But, Mark, actually what is *Creative Visualization?*"

He explained, "Well, as a matter of fact, I brought a copy of the book for you."

He went into the bedroom, reached into his luggage, and handed me the book.

"Knowing your inquisitive mind," he teased, "you will enjoy this book and find it most enlightening."

I glanced through a few pages, thanked him, and said I would look at it more thoroughly after dinner.

He went on to describe how he was practicing *creative visualization* and *the power of the mind.* He explained that it had helped him in many ways during the course of his days.

I had no inkling, at that time, that his giving me that book would encourage me to study and practice the methods taught in the book. I was encouraged to study and practice the philosophies in the book, and it was Mark's way of preparing me, guiding me for what was ahead—*the time to walk the path of devastation.*

By including me, giving me that book, Mark was better able to make his creative visualization an even more important part of his life.

The love, hope, devotion, admiration and support from his family and friends who were with him was so deeply necessary for Mark's survival. It gave him positive emotions and stimulated his healing process. He didn't allow negative or stressful thoughts, but instead, concentrated strongly on healing and recovery. His will to live and his practicing positive methods of self fulfillment fed the flames of his inner strength.

In a discussion about mind control, Bernie had said to Mark, "It is to say, and *believe* tomorrow will be better!"

But Mark corrected his father. "Most emphatically, NO!" he said as he slammed his fist on the table. "It is to say and believe . . . I *know* tomorrow will be better!"

CHAPTER FOUR

Hopes For Recovery

AIDS was beginning to show its devastating face in many ways in Mark's life during the summer of 1987. He was admitted to the New York University Medical Center Cooperative Care Unit twice, during July and August, for infections.

There, a patient is provided a private room and bath, twin beds, sitting area, television and a refrigerator. A spouse, or someone close to the patient, is permitted to sleep in the room with the patient and have meals together in the dining room. They can live in an atmosphere similar to a home environment.

As a patient there, Mark was not confined to his room. He was encouraged to shower, dress every day, and get out of the room. He had his own key. When it was time for treatments or exams, an announcement to report to the doctor's office came over the intercom.

Edmund moved in with Mark. The room became their home away from home. Many a day, Mark would get permission for Bernie and I to lunch with him in the dining room. Afterward, we often sat in the solarium and enjoyed the soothing effects of the East River, the sun streaming through the windows, and someone playing a piano at the far end of the room.

Mark would often tell us, "Mom, Dad, I'm so lucky to have you two."

One day he said, "See that guy sitting at the desk with the nurse? He has AIDS. The other day, after you left, he came over and asked if you were my parents. He sees you with me almost every day, and he made it a point to tell me how *grateful* I should be to have such loving, caring and supportive parents.

"I told him, *You don't have to tell me that. I know it and I love them dearly.* His parents never visited him, although they called once in a while. I want you to meet him. His name is Ken."

We met Ken and invited him to have lunch with us. It was good for all of us.

The hospital's approach is that if a patient lives in a homelike atmosphere, healing is helped—physically and psychologically. Mark was often given a pass to leave the hospital and have dinner out with us, Edmund, and other friends. At times, we asked Ken to join us.

Mark felt very comfortable at the hospital. At times he conducted business from his room by telephone or had one of his staff spend the afternoon with him, going over paper work, exchanging ideas, or discussing new clients or how to handle his present clients.

Bernie and I would sit and listen, happy to be with our son.

With Mark's treatments, his mental attitude and optimism, he beat the odds. He was home and back to work by the end of August, functioning normally in every aspect. *The eternal optimist!*

He would often say, "Mom, as I have told you before, I'm doing great. I'll get another infection. I'll beat it, then another and another. I'm on top of everything, all treatments, old and new. Plus, I take AZT.

I make it top priority to receive up-to-the-minute reports through the People With Aids Coalition (PWA), plus Project Inform."

He went on to expound about Project Inform, located in San Francisco. "Because our government and the U.S. Food and Drug Administration (FDA) are dragging their ass, Project

Inform—through the underground organizations—works to keep up to date with any new drug coming out of research from all over the world. They pursue developments relentlessly and pass the information on to patients."

Not knowing what each day was going to bring forth was getting to me, physically and mentally. I was becoming a nervous wreck, inside and outside.

Early in September we met Mark and Edmund for dinner in Manhattan. All through dinner I did not take my eyes off my son. When we were leaving the restaurant, Edmund whispered to me, "Sylvia, I have been watching you. You haven't taken your eyes off Mark. He is doing fine. You see how well he looks. He has even gained a few pounds. Don't worry!"

I admitted Edmund was right.

A few days later, during one of our many conversations on the telephone, Mark suggested, "Get in touch with an AIDS support group for parents who have children with AIDS. There is a branch not far from where you live. My friend's parents attend the meetings."

"Thanks, Son. I'll call and get the lowdown."

"Mom, I think it will be good for the both of you, sharing and talking with people in the same boat."

I called and found that particular group completely pessimistic. Their basic concept was to prepare yourself for bereavement. Not for me! I rejected that philosophy and began to think as Mark did. *Optimistic! Power of Mind! Meditation! Creative Visualization!* And, I read and reread.

I also practiced the New Age theories—mind, body and healing. At one point, I asked Mark if he would give me permission to speak with his doctor.

"Of course, Mom," he answered, "if it will make you feel better."

Mark gave me the doctor's telephone number and said, "I'll tell him you're going to call." I wanted questions answered that I knew I could not ask Mark.

The doctor was not available when I first called, but the young man on the phone sensed my nervousness and asked if perhaps he could help.

"I'm Mark Jollie," he said. "I work closely with the doctor."

When I told him who I was and why I was calling, he immediately put me at ease.

"Yes, Mark told me you would call. I want you to feel comfortable with me. Ask me anything you want. I'm sure I'll be able to answer your questions. Don't hesitate to let me know if you would rather speak with the doctor."

His attitude was so reassuring, and he was so knowledgeable and capable, I felt no need to speak with the doctor. He took time and his compassion and understanding helped quiet my nerves. We spoke for quite a while.

"Take my home phone number," he offered, " and call any time you feel the need." I did call him, and he was a constant source of relief, always there for me.

I also researched *homosexuality* and learned everything possible about AIDS. I wanted to find out, for myself, everything in depth.

I called Project Inform in San Francisco and found that what Mark had told me about them was correct. They gave me comfort. I asked to be put on their mailing list. Most importantly, by receiving current information directly from the source, I was keeping stress and strain off Mark by not having to question him about the latest research data. Any time I called, they were kind and cooperative. Every question was answered clearly and with patience.

I learned of experiments and research going on in different countries, which have not been acknowledged in the United States. Researchers all over the world have been working on their own theories, with acceptable results. Experiments, yes, but a last there are smitherings of hopes.

Israel has a promising treatment called *A/L 721*. Despite pressure from AIDS patients and their families to expedite approval, FDA has thrown up roadblocks to prevent the use of A/L 721 in this country. Our bureaucracy in full action!

AZT is being brought into the U.S. from Mexico at a pittance of its extremely high price in the U.S. Meantime, AIDS cases have increased by thousands—and homosexual cases are decreasing, while heterosexual cases are increasing.

With my life in turmoil, duality of thoughts running through my head, fighting to be optimistic, I was unable to sleep through many nights. I was up at all hours, listening to late night radio talk shows. One night, as I turned the dial, I picked up Barry Farber, who was talking about AIDS.

He was telling about an AIDS patient who had gone to Israel for treatment. A doctor at the Weizmann Institute of Science, a scientific institute at Rehovot, Israel, had discovered an immunity boosting agent which came to be called A/L 721.

It is not a drug, but a nutritional product derived from eggs. Farber announced that the young man, who was at death's door, had heard about Israel's find and made the trip there in a wheelchair.

Weeks later, he was back home in the United States, progressing very well. After he appeared on the Barry Farber show to tell the world about A/L 721, Barry Farber, being most skeptical, sent his daughter, a writer, to Israel to confirm the miracle development.

I sat up in bed, intently listening to every word, with pencil and paper in hand.

I called Barry Farber first thing the next morning to get his opinion of all this. I told him about my son and I asked, "Where can I get A/L 721?"

He had no answers for me at the time. He was waiting for his daughter to return from Israel a few days later. At that time, he planned to report her findings.

Emotionally wound up, I stayed close to the radio for days. I did not say a word to Mark until I could give him some secure thoughts.

My patience wore thin and I phoned Barry Farber again. All he could tell me was that his daughter could not yet confirm anything the young man had said about Israel having A/L 721.

He had spoken to his daughter on the phone and he hoped to have something to tell his audience once she returned home.

It was much too important not to pursue this. I tried calling a doctor at the institute in Israel, but to no avail.

I traced down the young man on Barry Farber's program. He gave me his mother's telephone number.

They lived in Jersey, not too far from where we were living. We had long telephone conversations. She gave me all the data and convinced me Israel was the place for my son to be.

Once I had some conclusive evidence, I called Mark. By that time, Bernie and I had decided we were taking our son to Israel for A/L 721 treatments.

I arranged for Mark and Edmund to come for dinner the following Sunday. I gave them a complete update on our findings.

"Mark, Dad and I feel A/L 721 is hopeful. We're making plans to take you to Israel at once. We have already updated our passports, so please make sure your passport is up to date."

Mark said, "Hold on just a minute! I know all about this A/L 721 through the underground. I did not say anything because I did not want to raise your hopes. I am on the waiting list!

"It should come through in about three or four weeks. I was going to tell you, once I received it." Then Mark started to laugh.

"Knowing you, Mom, I should have realized, you don't let any grass grow under your feet."

"Is it coming from Israel?" I questioned.

"No way! It costs a fortune that way. Our underground is having it made up for us for next to nothing, right here in New York."

"But, Son, I also found out it has to be pure, and that the exact amount of each part must be mixed properly or else it could kill you.

"And, Mark, if we can get you help in Israel now, you will be weeks ahead of the game. I learned that South Africa also has A/L 721. I'll take you any place in the world for help. I'll move heaven and earth, beg, borrow or steal and do everything possible. My son is not going to die because of AIDS!"

"I love you," he answered, "for everything you are doing, but, Mom, Dad, I know what I'm doing. The A/L 721 is being processed by experts. I don't have to travel any place to get the help I need. Let me do it my way."

I didn't want to place any unnecessary stress on him and from the tone of his voice, I knew it was best to back off.

He did get the A/L 721, just as he said he would.

He was doing nicely, with no signs of infection. Bernie and I remained up north as long as possible in the event Mark had to return to the hospital. We returned to Florida in late October.

Because of the events of the past months, I went into a state of emotional fatigue. The optimism Mark had instilled in me slowly dwindled away. My only thought was that I was going to lose my son.

I was becoming more and more emotionally out of control. I could not eat, I lost much weight, I cried constantly. I withdrew from my invigorating morning walks and disconnected myself from all social engagements. I ignored any responsibilities of homemaking.

My husband took over all tasks, plus constantly encouraged me. He repeatedly reminded me, "Sylvy, dear, you must get hold of yourself. Fight this! You are strong, so don't let Mark down. Remember, he is coming down for the holidays. You must not let him see you like this. It is not good for him."

I knew Bernie was right. I finally consented to see our doctor for a complete physical examination.

I told my doctor everything—the gloom, the doom and the pending disaster in our lives.

"Now, Sylvia," he said with concern, "you are in good shape, physically. But, if you don't make an honest, sincere attempt to pull yourself together, *stress* might kill you.

"The very first thing you must do," he continued, "is go for counseling, for your sake, the family's sake and especially for Mark. He needs you to be strong. You must make every effort to get up and out, to continue with your life. Your son is not giving up, not allowing this terrible disease to ruin his life. You are a strong lady, and I know you can do it."

He prescribed a tranquilizer and an antidepressant. I listened and slowly forced myself back to my usual routines.

I told Bernie, "*Deja vu* ten years ago. Dealing with homosexuality, you were the one who needed help. Now, it is my turn for the need. *Role reversal.*"

Early in the mornings, I once again took my cardiovascular walks. I saw a counselor once a week. Bernie and I went to Recovery Inc. meetings once or twice a week. Mental Health Through Will-Training, Recovery Inc., is a community mental health organization that offers a self-help method of will training. The recovery method is a system of techniques for controlling temperamental behavior and changing attitudes toward nervous systems and fears.

Recovery offers no quick and easy method which will immediately banish nervous symptoms and fears. However, those who have patiently practiced Recovery's self-help method, and have participated regularly in the group meetings, have proven that the Recovery method really works. Recovery helps you to help yourself.

In weekly group meetings, which last about two hours, members help each other by giving samples of how they have practiced the Recovery method in facing and handling specific difficulties. The meetings are conducted by veteran members who have received extensive leadership training.

Recovery does not supplant the physician. Each member is expected to follow the authority of his own physician or other professional. The Recovery method offers training in self-help and self leadership. It does not offer advice, diagnosis, treatment or counseling.

Recovery Inc. was organized in 1937 by a small group of patients of the late Abraham A. Low, M.D., Associate Professor of Psychiatry at University of Illinois Medical School. Dr. Low developed the Recovery techniques after many years of research, study, and treatment of patients. The self-help method is based on Dr. Low's book, *Mental Health Through Will Training*. Recovery is an adult program for persons 18 years of age or more. There is no charge, and it is nonprofit.

Our sons were very proud of us when they learned their Mom and Dad were invited to become leaders in Recovery Inc.

II.

**"Man's Inhumanity to Man
Makes Countless Thousands Mourn!"**

Mark Twain

Letters From the Earth (Harper and Rowe 1974)

CHAPTER FIVE

Unlock The Closet

I saw an article in the local newspaper discussing the start of an AIDS support group, headed by Terry Villaire, Employee Assistant Program Coordinator at the Boca Raton Hospital. He and Barbara Whiteside, a nurse who had just lost a son to AIDS, decided to start the group, which includes people whose relatives have AIDS—their sons, daughters, brothers, sisters and others. AIDS patients also attend the group's meetings.

At the first meeting Bernie and I attended, the group sat in a circle for about 30 to 45 minutes, very openly discussing our feelings, actions, and reactions. We talked about the latest medical findings, hoping our exchange of knowledge was helpful to each other. The support we gave to each other was reassuring. We also cried together and laughed together.

During the second part of the meeting, the patients went into a room with a social worker. However, any patient who preferred to stay in the family group could do so.

The AIDS-infected patients at these meetings usually do not have family living in Florida, and parents who attend often have AIDS-infected sons and daughters living in states other than Florida.

The group meets every Monday night at the hospital. We hug *hello* and we hug *'til we meet again.*

It has been in these meetings that I learned of the appalling lack of humanity existing in our world today—lack of love, support, compassion and caring by parents, even though these human compassions are sorely needed by AIDS patients. There are parents who have estranged themselves from their own flesh and blood because their child, no matter what age, has AIDS.

As the months went by, Bernie and I developed a special rapport with some of these forsaken young people. We socialized with them and are their surrogate parents. They grew to know Mark through our conversations and always inquired about his health. Mark, in turn, knew them through us.

Our children, Paul, Mark, and Edmund, have been ecstatically pleased with our participation in groups. And by sharing our feelings with others, we all can cope better.

Humanity must care! It is almost certain that someone in your life—it might be a relative or a friend will come down with AIDS. Likely, they will be subjected to a nightmare of discrimination, plunged into poverty by the cost of medical treatment and loss of employment. Their family, friends, and colleagues will reject them and they will face disability and death alone.

To avoid family and public disapproval, AIDS patients tend to keep their condition a secret and handle their grief and fear in isolation. This can intensify feelings of resentment and rebellion, and result in divisive or destructive behaviors in families who need *now* more than ever to pull together.

The foundation of our humane society rests upon our determination to care for our loved ones who are ill. Neglecting to understand their needs and provide what is required to meet these needs calls into question our claim to be a *civilized society.* Today, our society is out of step with reality!

Humanistic parents create love, compassion, and acceptance. They care and they are there to nurture. They willingly share the most precious and painful aspects of their child's life.

36

They can understand the language of the unspoken word and the human heart.

And, sadly, there are parents who create misery. To them I say, *Don't Do That To Your Child During The Most Needed Time of His or Her Life! This Is Your Very Own Flesh and Blood!*

It is time to unlock the closet door marked AIDS and emerge together holding hands. We need to nurture our children and ease the stress and anxiety for all. We need to make it easier for all to cope.

Being there tells them they are no longer alone, psychologically, physically or emotionally. Children and parents can face the future together with courage and hope.

At the AIDS Support Group, one young man in particular grabbed at the strings of my heart. Matt was a gem of a personality. Tall, dark, handsome, virile, he has deep, black expressive eyes, and he is also articulate, intelligent and talented. He is there for everyone and he is compassionate, supportive and loving, as well as the first to volunteer his services, day or night.

Matt usually sat with the family group during meetings, rather than going with the patients' group. He often called me between meetings, anxious to know about Mark. Bernie and I invited him to have lunch with us on occasion.

One afternoon after lunch, as we were leaving the restaurant, I suggested, "Matt, if you have the time, would you like to go to the beach and enjoy the coolness of the day?" Bernie and I had beach chairs in the trunk of the car.

"We often go to the beach to enjoy the smell of salt air and the blue-green water when it meets a clear blue sky on the far horizon. It is so conducive to calmness, peace and tranquility."

Matt answered, "That sounds terrific! I'm free for the rest of the afternoon."

At the beach we took off our shoes, rolled up our pants, and enjoyed the water as it rolled along the sand and cooled our feet. We carried an umbrella to protect ourselves from the hot Florida sun.

As we walked in the edge of the eternal sea, I told Matt, "We do this with our sons when they visit us."

It was in this soothing, relaxing, therapeutic atmosphere that Matt revealed to us his heart-breaking experience with his

37

mother. When he was 17, he told her he was *homosexual.* He told us of her incredible cruelty after his personal disclosure.

Since then, 25 years had gone by and he could still feel the pain of his mother grabbing him by the neck, pushing him against the wall and shouting, "Don't tell me you're a *fag!*" Then she screamed, "I don't want you living in the same house with me. Get out! Come back when you come to your senses."

Matt forgave her, but he will never forget the hurt and rejection she caused him.

Matt explained, "We were living in Rhode Island. I had just graduated from high school and was going to attend a local college while living at home. My father, however, was silent through all of this, and my 10-year-old sister was too young to understand.

"Afterwards, I contacted a homosexual friend who was going to college in Arizona. I left home quietly after telling my local friends I was taking a trip out west to visit with out-of-state friends.

"I worked my way through college in Arizona and built myself a career in architecture. I found a good job with an established company. I was content with my social and private life and I was accepted by heterosexual as well as homosexual friends."

He continued, "My contact with my family was minimal. Letters I sent to my mother came back marked RETURN TO SENDER.

"My sister was the *catalyst*. She managed to get my address off of one of the envelopes before my mother sent it back. Over the years, she visited with me secretly. In time, I achieved a partnership in a very highly respected organization. In 1987, I was diagnosed *AIDS Positive*. I was forced to give up my business because of medical and financial problems.

"My parents had retired to south Florida and my sister was married and living in north Florida. I rationalized, *I am living on borrowed time.* Now is the time I must re-unite with my family and live with love and respect among each other. Our past prejudice and disappointments must go beyond sweeping it under the rug."

Matt continued to tell us of his past as we waded in the cleansing water. "We must sweep it out of our lives. We must mend all fences. This can only be accomplished through close communication.

"I had no trouble making contacts for health services through friends and the People With Aids Coalition (PWA) in Florida. They helped me find an apartment in West Palm Beach."

As he told his story, Matt had become tense, and there was a tremor in his voice. I wanted to calm him, relax him.

"Matt," I said, "let's take a walk along the beach. The exercise will do us all some good."

He answered, "No, Sylvia, I'm okay," then he continued.

"The first time I visited my parents was very difficult for all of us—like strangers who meet in the night. My mother found it very hard to re-establish a relationship with me. I gave it much time, however. I visited often to have just casual talk and give us a chance to get to know each other again, and *to love* each other again. Gradually, I brought her up to date with my life.

We talked about all the years of my life we had been separated, what my life was like at the present time, my attitudes and my hopes.

"Sylvia," he interjected, "I'm dedicated to *wellness*. Just as your son, Mark, is not leaving it up to the doctors to fix it, I also am dedicated to fixing it myself."

Matt went on telling us about his family. "I told my mother how the stressfulness of the dichotomy of the family was taking its toll on me at that time in my life. I explained that my needs from them—mother, father and sister— would help all of us, psychologically and emotionally.

"But, I could not penetrate *that wall* my mother had built around herself. That was a *stunning* realization to a son."

Even though Matt's mother knew he had an incurable, devastating disease, she showed him no sign of love, support or compassion.

"Matt," I offered, "would you like for me to speak with your mother?"

"Thank you, but *no*," he answered. Nevertheless, Matt was determined and he continued to visit his parents.

Over the months ahead, however, Matt's condition continued to deteriorate and he had to be hospitalized. That was a turning point for his mother.

He explained, "I think that seeing the reality of what I went through in the hospital *struck* my mother. For the first time, she seemed to realized *I could die.*

"She started to ask all kinds of questions and to show some genuine concern. I sensed a feeling of emotion finally penetrating her wall."

After Matt's stay at the hospital, he was making arrangements to return to his apartment when, to his astonishment, his mother suggested, "Matt, why don't you stay at my house while you are recuperating? This way, you won't have to live alone."

Matt told us, "I gratefully accepted her offer. I knew in my heart *we* were on the way back to being a family again. I knew she was saying *Welcome Home!*"

With tears in his eyes and emotion in his voice, he continued to explain. "I have come full circle. Now, I am home."

At this writing, February 1990, Bernie and I have continued to see Matt. He is on an experimental drug, and he seems to be doing well enough. I'm sorry to say, though, he is not the vibrant, energetic young man of the past. I can see it in his eyes, and our hearts go out to him and his family.

I speak to his mother on the telephone, but we have never met. She is familiar with our relationship with Matt. How much he has told her about our family, I don't know.

I am so pleased this fine young man has found his family again and is living with them in psychological and emotional comfort. They are there for him. Matt's mother made a difference! Matt was extremely comforting to us when our son moved on to his peace.

Now, when I sit with the AIDS Support Group, listening to the devastating stories the patients openly tell about their families abandoning them—because of a quirk of fate that life handed them through no control on their part—I am so deeply grateful for the love, caring, devotion, compassion, support, and display of humanity our family shares.

I often think about a mother who sat with us, cried and begged for help. Her husband didn't want her to have anything to do with their son, who had AIDS. She was caught in the middle. To whom does she owe her allegiance?

And I think about a father who did not visit his ill son, and who, when the boy died, told everyone it was cancer. He did not attend the funeral.

There are more examples. Eve, another mother we know, had a friend since kindergarten, for 55 years. Her friend deserted her hysterically when she told her, "My son has AIDS."

When Sandy told his supposedly loving neighbor and friend, Pat, that his son had died of AIDS, Pat responded, "I don't want to be your friend anymore. You talk too much about AIDS and your son." Pat showed no compassion or understanding, even though talking is cathartic for Sandy, and helped ease his pain.

At another meeting I was told about Sarah. She deeply loved her brother, Bill, but their parents disowned him when they found out he was homosexual. They hated Sarah because she continued to see her brother. The fact that Bill has AIDS has not tempered his father's feelings, however, and he refers to Bill as *"The Fairy."*

Sarah loves, respects, and admires her brother and his companion, Bob. When she visits them, she sits on the club chair and they sit close on the couch. They kid and talk about this or that. She sits quietly, listens while they hold hands, plan what they're going to have for dinner, and discuss whose turn it is to do the cooking. She can see the intimacy between them, a warm bond of love and affection. Each of them completes the other. They are one and no strain shows. There is a privacy.

Sarah often thinks, "I hope some day to meet a man, marry, and have the relationship I see in them. I am learning from my homosexual brother and his companion that this is what life is all about—giving of each other to each other, not *gender*.

She worries much about Bob, however, because he has AIDS related complex (ARC).

41

CHAPTER SIX

Danny, Another Son and Brother

Author's Note: This chapter is the story of Ken Nickels and his long-time companion, Daniel Cadbas, as told to me, word for word. The original story was dictated by Ken Nickels.

Daniel Cadbas entered his world on a typical, cold Perry Lane, Vermont winter, windy day. It was bleak and dark. But for the Cadbas family, there wasn't anything *bleak* about it, that February 28,1943. For them, it was the brightest, warmest, most radiant, happiest day of their lives.

The entire small town was overjoyed with the new arrival, Daniel, a "change of life" gem. His mom was in her mid-40s and had previously given birth to four other fine children. Naomi, the oldest, was 24 years old. Teddy was 22, Barton 20, and Anne 18. Naomi later married Steve, and Teddy married Doria (a Massachusetts girl). Anne and Barton are unmarried.

Danny was a treasure, like a gift from God. He was very "babied" and catered to by everyone in and outside his family.

He was very young when his father became seriously ill with diabetes and required his mother's full-time attention.

At that time in the family history, Naomi took over the maternal obligations to "raise" Danny. However, he deeply loved his mother, but with his father being in and out of the hospital, he didn't see much of her. Danny missed her very much.

Danny's father's illness went on for a couple of years, and at one point, they had to amputate his leg at the knee. Some time later they had to amputate the same leg until only a stub was left.

The family suffered much over this, and Danny's father died while Danny was in his early teens.

Danny's mother rapidly deteriorated mentally and physically. She also died three months later.

Danny never seemed to accept his mother's death. He grieved and grieved. He loved her so much. Meanwhile, his sisters took over his upbringing and "mothered" him. This was especially true for Naomi.

After Naomi married Steve, they all lived together in the family home. Shortly after, Teddy married and moved to Massachusetts. For Danny, his sisters were the main part of the family. He loved them so much and would not do anything to hurt them.

When Danny was five years old, he already knew he was *different*, even though he did not understand what the difference was. As he grew older and played with boys and girls his age, he realized he was growing into his teen-age years, and he was confused about his *feelings*.

Danny's brother-in-law, Steve, recognized Danny's *homosexuality* and took advantage of it.

Steve abused Danny sexually by having Danny perform sexual acts on him. He "swore" Danny to *secrecy* and threatened, "If you say one word to anyone about this, I'll tell your sisters it's all your fault, and they'll never love you again."

Danny was so starved for love and he missed his mother so much that he was trapped by the threat.

Danny's older brother, Barton, also began to notice Danny was homosexual, and he too abused him sexually. These events are a very important part of Danny's story.

Of course, Danny never told anyone about the abuses and, as a consequence, it continued for a very long time.

Finally, Danny went to a Catholic priest in their small town. But, the priest told him, "Nothing can be done. It is a small town. You can't tell anyone here you are *gay* because they won't accept it. They won't understand.

" This will *kill* your sisters," the Priest told Danny. "They will never be able to face anyone in town again."

Danny loved his sisters too much to do anything to hurt them, so he allowed the abuse and sexual use of himself to continue; and, he soon became involved with a few married men in the town. It just kept going on and on.

Just looking at Danny's family, you would think of them as the *All-American Family*, and that they were *leaders* in their community. Danny's sisters were cheerleaders in high school and all that sort of thing.

However, Naomi conceived Steve's child, and it was a *Hush! Hush!* wedding.

Over the years, since the parents died, Naomi and Steve had six sons. Danny was close in age to the younger ones, and he "grew up" with them.

Danny never went to his mother's grave. He never fully accepted her death, and it bothered him the rest of his life. She had died around December 5th, as I remember, and every year—just before Thanksgiving, he would go into a crying period which lasted through Christmas. He associated his whole life with her at that time every year.

As he grew older, Danny traveled a lot. He went all over the world, but his sisters never left Vermont. In his travels he was always looking for something special to send home to them.

His younger sister, Anne, never had a boyfriend, so Danny had "his doubts" about her and what her *sexuality* was. He always wished he could talk to her about that; but, at the same time, he was afraid to tell her he was *homosexual*. Danny knew his sisters could not understand his situation.

Whenever he was back in Vermont, between his world travels, he would secretly involve himself with a few local married men. Even though they did not consider themselves to be gay, Danny knew they were.

When Danny went off to college in Boston, he started socializing with more gay persons. He found out he wasn't the only one, anymore, and he also felt he was still in a small town.

In Massachusetts, Danny didn't have to be all that quiet about it, but, he still could not tell his family—especially Naomi. He always seemed to accept her as his mother, and he would never take the chance of hurting his mother. That is the way he looked at it.

Danny went through his college years with a couple of lovers, and he kept in close contact with Naomi and Anne. They both continued to adore him.

To give you some history, I first met Danny in New York City in early 1977. We were immediately *together*. And, we stayed together for approximately 13 years, until his death.

Danny was always involved with his family; but, except for Barton and Steve, (and a few local married men), no one knew Danny was gay. And they didn't know about me.

Eventually, Danny and I moved from New York City to Palm Springs, California. We worked as an office manager team for an interior decorating company.

Eventually, Danny became nervous, tired, and got sick. He went for a check-up and found out he was HIV-positive. That was back in 1982, I believe.

That was very early in the appearance of AIDS in America, and most doctors were scared to death of any patients who tested HIV-positive. They didn't want to touch them!

In Danny's case, they sent him to the cancer hospital in Los Angeles, where they did lymph node tests on him which, by the way, didn't show that much HIV-positive.

Later, they finally found Danny was definitely HIV-positive, but they called it *AIDS*.

Well, this diagnosis frightened Danny to death! However, he never really accepted it. He was so calm about it, and he went on okay for about a year or so. Then he got pneumonia (PCP) and had to be rushed to Cedars Sinai Hospital in L.A.

There, the staff definitely diagnosed AIDS, and his nurses just freaked out and treated him absolutely terribly. They were afraid to enter his room, and no one there seemed to know how to handle him.

Cedars Sinai had not had any AIDS patients up to that time. Meanwhile, his experience there was "blowing Danny's Mind." He was not used to being treated that way. He always had a lot of friends and was always an easy person to deal with.

Finally, one nurse came around and talked to him. She apologized for the rest of her staff, and even for some of the hospital's doctors, for the rude treatment they were giving him. She let him know that outside his door there were big, red-lettered signs reading *PLEASE DON'T COME NEAR THIS DOOR.*

It was just horrible, you know. Of course, Danny also had some friends who would not come near him, early in the stage of AIDS knowledge. People were just frightened to death of the word *AIDS!*

Well, Danny finally got fairly well and they sent him home and he went back to work. But, he was starting to think, "I have AIDS and I am dying." Next, his insurance company found out he had been diagnosed as having AIDS.

Even though he had just changed his job and his insurance, Cedars Sinai apparently notified his insurance company that Danny had a "pre-diagnosed" illness which would be fatal, and that caused his new insurance company to cancel his policy.

At that time, the Aids Projects Los Angeles (APL) was just being formed, and they had an attorney who managed to have Danny's insurance reinstated. However, it was reinstated with a $3000 deductible, which was ridiculous.

Not only that, Danny kept turning in the medical bills and they kept writing back, *we do not cover that in your insurance.* Eventually, the insurance proved to be worth *nothing.* Meanwhile, we moved to Los Angeles.

Next, we decided to try LAC-USC Medical Center. There, AZT and some other experimental drugs were being tried on AIDS patients. Danny was one of the patients who took AZT,

47

on an experimental basis, under direction of Dr. Gill, one of the "big doctors" in AIDS diagnosis and treatment.

Danny became his special patient. It worked out better mentally, and so much better for Danny when he entered LAC-USC. There, he was treated so kindly, and he began to come to grips with his infection.

He realized he would have to tell his sisters, because he did not want to die and leave them with no understanding.

He knew there might be a bad reaction on their part, but he did not expect they would turn against him because he was gay and dying of AIDS.

Meanwhile, I kept telling him, "Danny, don't tell them! Please, don't tell them!"

I just knew what would happen before he told them anyway. They said, "We want nothing to do with you ever! People from Vermont don't have stuff like that happen to them!"

After telling him that, his sisters got on the phone and soon had the whole family involved. Danny's brother-in-law, Steve, called and told him, "You are not to upset your sisters. We don't want to hear from you anymore—ever. And we don't want to hear any more of your stories. Don't ever call us again!"

All of that was just devastating to Danny, who was thinking he was *dying*. He felt his whole family and all the love any of them had for him was gone.

They were more worried about themselves, and people in the small town who might think something about them, than they were about Danny. And they were worried about people finding out someone from Vermont had AIDS.

Danny never got over that destruction of love and he cried day after day. He would telephone them, but they would hang up on him. It was just a *horrible thing*. And it was all out of *fear*.

After Danny started taking AZT, he thought he would be cured. So, he wrote a post card to one of his sisters. Nothing was in it about AIDS. He wrote, "They found a treatment and it is helping me. I'm feeling better."

Well, his sister had a fit and had the brother-in-law call Danny and tell him, "Never, never ever write to the family again—especially on a post card! Somebody in the post office will read it and find out you have AIDS. Please don't ever call or try to talk to us again."

Danny felt everything he did was against him, even though he was getting good care as USC. He stayed in fairly good shape for about two and a half years or more, but he stayed under terrible stress because of his family.

Well, finally, he got real sick and had to go into the hospital. I thought I should call his family for him.

He could always talk to his sister-in-law, Doria, who was at that time divorcing his brother, Teddy. They had been living in Massachusetts during the preceding years.

Danny never was close to his brother, Teddy, but he was able to talk to Doria and tell her things. She always kept somewhat of a communication with the family in Vermont.

Doria and Teddy had two mentally retarded children, and they were not wanted by the main family.

For Danny, he wanted to get back the love from both his sisters. He wanted them to say they loved him again, but they could not do that for him.

When he went into the hospital, Doria sent flowers, but Danny thought they were from his other sister, Naomi. Why so?

He was getting dementia from his toxoplasmosis, so his mental condition was deteriorating. He was so happy, thinking Naomi had sent the flowers, that he wouldn't let the nurses get near them.

I tried telling him that it was Doria, his sister-in-law, who had sent the flowers, but I could not get through to him.

He brought the flowers home after he was discharged from the hospital, and they just sat for months on a table near him before finally just falling all over.

He still did not have any communication with the family in Vermont. Meanwhile, through his sister-in-law, he heard that his brother, Teddy, had a heart attack and died. Danny wanted to go the funeral, but he was too sick. He called Vermont to tell his family he was coming anyway, but they demanded he not come.

Doria and Teddy's retarded children knew about Danny, and they had been warned not to say anything to anyone at the funeral. They were told to not even mention Danny's name.

49

The fact that Danny was gay and had AIDS kept him from knowing his six nephews. Doria once told Danny she suspected one of her boys was gay, and this caused Danny to have a desperate need to talk to the boy. But he dared not, because he was afraid that would hurt his sister, Naomi. Danny backed off and ignored the whole situation.

In the interim, before Teddy had died, Dan found the opportunity to tell Teddy that he was homosexual and was dying from AIDS. Teddy accepted it, but never told the family. Teddy accepted it because he knew he had a bad heart condition and that his time was short.

Danny started to go in and out of the hospital, constantly having one attack of AIDS after another. His need for his family became stronger, and he wanted to connect with them. I called Doria and told her, "Danny is dying and he is desperate. He is in such despair. He needs to see some family before he dies."

She relayed the information to the remaining brother, Barton, but nobody wanted to come and see Danny. Nobody wanted to connect with him as family.

So anyway, Danny survived for another year. He went on living, a long-term survivor. At one point, the doctors called me in their office and told me Danny was really near death, that he must see his family. The doctors explained, "That is what is keeping him alive—the need to see his family—even though he is suffering terribly."

At that point in time, Danny told me he had asked one of his sisters if he could be buried next to their mother. "No way," she answered. "With AIDS, you're not wanted in Vermont. And we don't want you near Mother."

That night, I decided to call the sisters and plead for Danny to be buried near his mother. This became a real horrible situation, far more than I can explain, back and forth, back and forth.

Doria finally told me they discussed that Danny should be buried where he and I lived, in California, and that I was supposed to take care of everything. They said if I would let them know when he died, the brother and brother-in-law would come out for the funeral.

I told Doria I need her help. I once again told her Danny wanted to be buried near his mother. I didn't think they had the right to prevent that, and that it would have to go a little farther than just their *say so*.

Doria did not care if it caused a *Big Scene*. She let Steve and Barton know that she was going to make a big scene, and ·let Danny get what he wanted—to be brought back to Vermont.

It seemed that everyone in Vermont had to get involved. I got no where, and not a word from anyone. Finally, the night came when the doctor told me Danny would die within hours.

I went home, called his sisters and told them I had to make burial arrangements. I asked them what I should do. I had never dealt with death. It was all new to me. I had no support and no family to go to myself. I was frightened.

His sister yelled over the telephone, "He is not being buried here! He is not coming back here!"

I screamed back at her, "Put your husband on the telephone. I've got to talk to someone who doesn't tell me it can't be done."

I got Steve on the telephone and told him, "I'll make a scene out of this. I will go to the Aids Project Los Angeles (APLA) and tell this story. It will become a real big problem to you, because they are *looking* for stories like this."

So, Steve said he would go to the city hall and find out if Dan could be buried near his mother. Because Danny had AIDS, Steve planned to do so *on the quiet*.

The decision was that if Danny was cremated and placed in a sealed urn, he could be buried in the small town graveyard next to his mother. All of this was because of the fear of AIDS. Uneducated stupidity! A little graveyard that probably has no legal aspects. They made a big deal out of it because of the fear of AIDS!

Steve was showing some extra fear, and he knew what I was talking about when I told him, "I know lots of things that went on in Danny's life when he was small and lived in Vermont. Now, I want him buried next to his mother, or I will bring out everything!"

51

Steve then answered, "I will take care of it. I'll do what I can do."

He knew exactly what I meant. They were the ones who said nothing like homosexuality happened in Vermont, yet it had gone on in their very own family for years.

He suddenly became very cooperative and even called me back later that night. "Yes," he explained, "arrangements have been made. He can be buried in the graveyard with his mother."

I called Doria and told her, "At least I've gotten this far. If he is cremated, and of course I can get Danny to sign the papers for cremation, he can be buried in the same graveyard as his mother."

Danny and I had never really talked about burial during our years together. He just wanted to be buried near his mother. We talked about cremation only briefly.

Danny didn't die that night. It was another time when he became alert and came home from the hospital.

Soon after, he got a call from his sister, who was still trying to get him buried in California. She wanted him to say he would never come back to Vermont. But Danny didn't know what she was talking about because he had *toxoplasmosis*. His sister couldn't get anything clear with him about the burial.

Finally, a day or so later, Naomi called and wanted to talk to me. Danny understood that. He and I were always able to communicate, even though he wasn't able to communicate with other people.

Naomi was very mad and became very nasty. "How dare you tell us he is dying when he wasn't?"

They were ignoring the whole death process. They didn't know what I was going through, attending to his every need, taking care of him, cleaning up after his diarrhea. And I wasn't asking them for any help. I loved Danny.

The hospital had sent him home because they didn't have room for him anymore in the AIDS ward. Danny's family just had no idea what I was going through.

They were throwing all of it on me, like the burial was some kind of game. I told Naomi, "Don't you ever talk to me like that again. I won't ever talk to you again. I'll talk to your husband, and he knows why!"

52

She started yelling into the telephone, blaming me for Danny's death, but I'm not even infected. He got sick four or five years after we began living together.

Anyway, Danny lived for several months after that. Meanwhile, no one in the family called to find out anything. I knew I needed somebody to talk to because I knew I would have to be able to bury Danny and that I would need to know what to do at the last minute.

I kept in touch with Doria, who promised "Danny will be buried next to his mother. I'll see to it that it will be done."

During Danny's thinking of his dying, he started to talk about a marker. I thought, "Oh! What now? God! Now another problem. He wants some sort of marker!"

Again, Doria assured me it would be done. She let me know she knew what had taken place between her two brothers-in-law and Danny, many years before.

Next, Danny went to a hospice. He became able to talk again and came *back to life*. Strange! He started talking about his sisters again, real alert. I told him it was too late, and that I didn't want to deal with them at that point.

Suddenly, Danny deteriorated. He couldn't move his body, he couldn't talk.

When I left the Chris Brownlie Hospice in Los Angeles that night, I told Danny, "I'll be back tomorrow." Apparently, he could hear me because he squeezed my hand. When I walked into his room the next day, the nurses were there and said, "He is dying and probably won't last much longer. But he's hanging on, waiting for you to get here."

Sure enough, Danny knew when I came in. The nurses explained that he could hear, but couldn't respond. He was gasping for breath. They left me alone with him. His family wasn't dealing with it and friends couldn't help any more.

Luckily, I had met this lady reverend, Sandy Scott, the night before at a Louise Hay spiritual meeting. She helps dying AIDS patients. She is with the non-sectarian United Spirit Church of Hollywood, California.

She told me if I needed any support, to call her, so I asked the Chris Brownlie Hospice to get in touch with Reverend

Sandy Scott. They knew of her, and they immediately called her. She came right over.

She told me, "Yes, he's dying, getting ready to go." She talked to him. He was lying in the room where the sunlight was coming right in on him. She told him to look into the light. He responded to her suggestion. She told me, "I'm going to leave you two together."

She told Danny one more time to look directly into the light, then said to me, "His breathing is shifting. I have to leave the room. You are going to have to be with him."

Sure enough, Danny's breath became very shallow and it just went real smooth. All of a sudden, he went. That was it. The last breath. And I knew it was. I kind of screamed and Reverend Scott walked in and knew it was all over.

I went home and called the family in Vermont. They were all very calm and actually thanked me for calling. That is all they said, however. Nothing more. They said nothing about the funeral.

I had made the cremation arrangements the day before and everything was together. It worked out.

The family, however totally ignored his death. I called them again and told them, "Let me tell you one thing. His body has already been taken care of. He is now being cremated and he is coming back to Vermont. It is set up and he is on his way to where he wants to be."

His sister, whom Danny loved like a mother, just hung up the telephone.

I went to the crematorium and told them, "I want to be sure everything is proper." They verified that a black marble container was acceptable, properly sealed. It was to be sent immediately to Vermont with Danny's ashes inside. Danny's *remains*.

Doria had said she would let me know when the burial would take place.

Danny died April 9, 1990. As of August 1990, the black marble urn was still sitting in the city hall. The family refused to have it buried next to Danny's mother. I had the urn shipped to them because I figured one day somebody will see that Danny gets buried next to his mother.

Doria called and said if they have to do it themselves, the remains will be placed next to their mother.

In September 1990, Doria called to tell me she had just returned from Vermont. She had a long, private talk with Steve and Barton. While she was there, Danny was buried between his mother and his father.

May he rest in peace and have the peace and love he never had in life. Danny, I love you and miss you.

Steve and Barton will always live in fear, for their past sins against Danny will always haunt them. Will these sins be revealed? Will the town ostracize them as they helped ostracize Dan?

The family still tells everyone Danny died of a heart attack.

III. AIDS Thrives on Silence

From A Medical Doctor, About Humanistic Needs

Relieve the stress and strain of your son or daughter who has AIDS! Reacting to your AIDS child with love, devotion, compassion, acceptance and understanding is of *utmost importance to their survival*. The Flow of positive love and emotion emanating from parent to child gives the offspring the *psychological moment* — the moment when the mind is willing to accept the knowledge that the child is accepted by his or her parents.

Satisfying this deep feeling and emotion, this desperate need for moral support, this moment when the mind is willing to accept, is *most critical*. This love gives strength. The mind reacts in the affirmative. The inner will to fight off the disease comes from this love and understanding of the positive thoughts, feelings and actions of the parents. Knowing of the love, the empowering *WILL* and the *POWER* of the *MIND* telling themselves, "I can now accomplish what I want."

The *HUMAN* response of this love from the parents conveys this message into his or her mind and helps them fight for survival and *wellness* of thought. The desire for living is reinforced. The hopes, desires and energies stored within the son or daughter will keep them fighting for a longer life.

We all think this cannot happen to us. But, we must be prepared, as parents and children, for we all are vulnerable to becoming involved with AIDS — directly or indirectly — and we all are subject to being affected — psychologically, physically and emotionally if this happens, the *now touched* and the *now untouched*.

The humanistic need for parent and child must be fulfilled, free of all doubt and anxiety. The need for the humanistic connection must become known to all peoples. The *person with AIDS* (PWA), must know he or she is accepted and loved. Education and public awareness are keys to understanding. Humanity toward all mankind is the answer. Unconditional Love Makes the Difference!

Dr. Martin Kleiman
Professor of Infectious Diseases
Riley Hospital for Children - Indianapolis, Indiana

One Person Will Make A Difference!
I Know! I Made A Difference!

REACH OUT . . .

To Your Child . . . Touch! Hug! Kiss!

With Care . . . Love! Support! Compassion!

Be There . . . Understand! Accept the Great Need!

Turn Despair . . . Into HOPE!

Be With Them . . . This Makes a Difference!

Say, "I Love You" . . . And Make A Big Difference!

CHAPTER SEVEN

Love, Letters and Interviews

Weeks after our beloved son departed this planet, Bernie and I debated with ourselves whether or not to return to the AIDS Support Group. We wondered how our presence might affect other parents who had children living *on the edge of death*. We wondered if we might cause them to think, "Sylvia and Bernie lost their son. Will my child be next?"

Confronted with this duality of thoughts, we came to the decision to follow the advice of Terry Villaire, the group leader. He recommended we continue to attend.

At the next meeting, we arrived early. As we waited for meeting time, I was reading a booklet on AIDS which I had picked up from a table. I was about half-way through the booklet when the door opened and I looked up to see a young man I had never seen before. He had difficulty walking, and was leaning heavily on his cane.

He was about six feet tall and had a dark complexion and black eyes. I guessed he was about 40 years old. He sat down along side of Bernie and me.

"Good evening," he said. "I'm Jack. Are you new here? I don't think I've seen you here before." It had been a while since Bernie and I had been to a meeting.

I introduced us. "My name is Sylvia, and this is my husband, Bernie. We are not *new* members. We just haven't attended meetings for the last couple of months. We lost our son, Mark, to AIDS in December."

Jack offered sincere condolences, then explained, "I have AIDS too. I just began attending these meetings. I don't come often. In fact, this is the first time in about three weeks.

Jack immediately opened up to us about the status of his condition. I felt an instant *chemistry* between us. He was charming, easy to talk to, and the *sensations* and *vibrations* between us grew stronger and stronger. I wondered *why?*

As other members of the group streamed in, our moments of comradeship were interrupted. Later, during a five-minute break, I asked Jack, "Have you met Matt?" and I said, "He is such a fine young man. I thought he might be here tonight."

Jack answered, "Yes, we've met and we like each other."

When, during the second half of the meeting, most of the persons with AIDS to be in their group, Jack stayed with Bernie and me. After the meeting was over, we walked him to his car.

As he got in, he asked, "Sylvia, Bernie, do you mind giving me your telephone number? I want to know about your son. In our talking tonight, I didn't have time to ask. Did you say his name was *Mark?*"

I replied, "Yes! His name is Mark, and no, we don't mind." I took paper and pen from my purse and wrote it down for him. "I deeply appreciate your interest," I added. "It is very thoughtful of you. Why don't you give us your phone number too? Perhaps Matt, Bernie and I can get together with you for lunch one of these days."

Still, the sensations and vibrations which surrounded me seemed mutual. He enthusiastically replied, as he took the handwritten note from my hand, "That suits me fine. I've been in Florida for only a few months, and I really don't know many people here. I live alone."

As I handed him the piece of paper upon which I had written our full first and last names, address and telephone number, Jack glanced at it only momentarily before a stunned look crossed his face. He shouted, "*Goldstaub! Goldstaub! Mark Goldstaub is your son?*"

Jack continued, excitedly. "I knew Mark. He and I had mutual friends. I've been to his office and to his home. He handled himself with such *dignity* during his battle with AIDS.

"He had courage, and his strength was awe-inspiring to everyone who knew him. Believe me, Sylvia and Bernie, your son was well-known and loved by everyone. He was truly a *humane* being. You should be so very proud of him, and I'm so very proud to know both of you!"

I wondered how such strange meetings, as ours with Jack, happen. Out of the blue, I suppose. We were simply attending a meeting and he showed up. We immediately developed a *rapport*, not knowing of his background.

I wondered if Mark's *spiritual energy* was surrounding me, and would always be with me. I wondered if he had guided this particular meeting, on this particular night, in order for us to meet his friend, Jack. I wondered if it was feasible that Mark had *brought us together because he knew Jack was alone.*

My intuition told me *yes*. I felt that a now *supernatural being*, Mark, had arranged this meeting between Jack, Bernie and me. The reasons for my earlier sensations and vibrations suddenly became obvious.

As he was so *humane in life on this earth*, Mark's humane spirit was prevailing on his present planet. Constant concern for his fellow man was always one of his trademarks. Some of the following letters from friends will testify further to his wonderful character:

August 1989

Dear Sylvia and Bernie,

I have wanted for such a long time to share with you my thoughts about Mark. I have been reluctant, for my sake, not yours. In the three years that I spent with Mark, he became *very important* to me. Consequently, it hurts me very much to think about those days.

First of all, I got the job with Mark through a mutual friend. I had been a waitress for 20 years and I wanted to branch out into something else, since I'm no longer in my "first youth." Mark was very busy. Actually, I don't have a clue as to what he was thinking when he hired me. I did not know how to do office work and I had absolutely no knowledge of the P.R. business. The type job that I had with Mark is actually a very sought-after position, particularly by "young kids" just out of college—communications majors, etc. To that end, you could easily say that I was very *lucky* to get the job.

At the end of my first day, Mark gave me a bouquet of flowers with a note saying how happy he was to have me as a member of the Mark Goldstaub Public Relations Family. Is that Incredible? Yes?

Well, I could give you a 50-page document about all the wonderful days and nights, but I'll try to keep it down to just the few really memorable things in my mind.

The publicity business is so *high-stress* that you would hardly believe it. You can *never* please the producers and you can *never* please the media. So, STRESS! At the end of many of those horrendous days, Mark would say, "Come on kids! Let's go have a drink." Or, he might say, "Let's all go to the movies!" Mark always had a little something extra to make you feel appreciated and really loved.

Sometimes, when a producer was particularly *vicious*, Mark would get mad at us. He'd rant and rave and holler and say we were *not communicating enough information to him*. He'd fume and fuss and storm out, slamming the door on the way. But—you could count on it—he would go out, ring for the elevator, and then while he was waiting for it, *change his mind*. He would come back to our office, stick his head in the door and say, "You guys are the best! I don't know what I'd do without you. I couldn't run this business without you." This happened every time.

Mark never really would leave the building without affirming that he appreciated us. That was the point in his organization—he cared about us, and he made that clear at all times.

Where can you get that, in the world we live in today? In most cases, not even in families. Mark would always tell us that he was trying to be careful not to treat us the way any of his employers had treated him. I never had to ask him for a raise. They were *offered*, and each time, I received more than I expected.

He was the president of the company, and he was a high-class executive—not only in name, but by nature. However, any request for us to do work was preceded with, "Could you do me a favor?" or he might say, "I hate to ask you this, but do you think you could . . .?"

All our jobs, large and small, when submitted, were accepted by him with, "Thanks! This is wonderful." All mistakes were treated as a matter of taste. He'd always say, "Maybe it would be better if we did it this way." There were never any recriminations. *Never.*

I was a horror! I had no experience. I knew nothing. I fumbled and fouled and Mark would say, "You are the best." I moaned and groaned and complained for the entire first three years. I'd say I *was quitting* or that *I hated the job*, and Mark would say, "You're right! It is a lousy business, but *you're so good at it!*"

We'd have parties for no logical reason. Mark would buy us gifts for no reason. We'd gossip, and we'd laugh!

I was the only woman on his staff, and when I'd complain that they were all *chauvinistic,* Mark would call me at home to thank me for reminding them that they should be careful about how they treated women.

When clients would complain about any of us, he'd risk losing the client to defend us to the last word. He never lost a client, however, because they respected his judgment so much.

I would never be where I am today, career-wise, if it were not for Mark Goldstaub. I learned so much from him. He *shared all his knowledge* and encouraged me to get our own clients, and use his name and facilities to accommodate our clients.

He was truly a *humane being*. I miss him more than these few words can express.

Love always,
Virginia

Dear Mr. and Mrs. Goldstaub,   December 22, 1988
    I resumed contact with Mark in early 1987 when I encountered him in the subway. My first thought was, "What a good-looking guy." That was before I realized he was actually someone I knew! We talked a lot and he took me to lunch at the Hyatt, across from my office, shortly thereafter. We spoke on the phone every couple of months. All this is background for the following statement:
    I have never had such inspirational, uplifting talks with anyone as I have with Mark, even after he told me what was going on health-wise with him. Not once did he sound bitter, despairing or afraid. Even the shock and sadness, which I couldn't help feeling, were welcome in our talks. Instead of being down, Mark was always Up!
    His attitude was so positive, and he was always making plans so he could make the most of his life, every day. And, he encouraged me to do the same. He always remembered from one talk to the next what problems I had mentioned the last time, and he made sure to ask about them specifically. He always wanted to know about my family, how my mother and sister were doing, about my kids, my new husband, my eating and exercise program (to lose weight) and other concerns about my life.
    I wish someone would tell me what gave Mark the courage and strength to step outside his problem and continue to live his life in such a positive fashion! I could use a shot of it myself! It's a scary world out there, sometimes.
    I know as his parents you must be going through the worst kind of heartache now. I hope it will help a tiny bit someday to look back on this letter and realize what I'm sure you already know—that your son grew into a handsome, thoughtful, caring person who enriched the lives of everyone who knew him, even just "phone pals" like me.
                    My best wishes to you both,
                    Mary Ellen White

This letter is from Mark's Cousin Myron:

December 22, 1988

Dear Aunt Syl and Uncle Bernie,

Although you may think everything that might have been said about Mark has already been said, I believe the best is yet to come.

The wonderful "uplifting" experience of those touching tributes to Mark, so beautifully articulated by those whom he loved and worked with, caused everyone to look at their own lives and see how well he or she measured up to Mark's shining example.

Everyone who was present will forever carry that challenge with them from now on, and I'm sure Marks' influence on many people's lives will help to significantly improve them, especially in the area of interpersonal relationships, where Mark obviously *excelled*.

As Mark may have once said, "Don't worry, be happy and just keep dancing, no matter how hard it gets."

All my love,
Myron

Mark's personal feelings about his battle with AIDS can best be described in his own words, as recorded and transcribed in this chapter, by Mike Greenly, who has graciously allowed the inclusion in this book his personal interview with Mark at University Hospital, in New York City. The interview initially began with a question addressed by Mike to Dr. Ron Grossman, who was Mark's long-standing, primary physician.

*****

Thursday, September 22, 1988

MIKE: Ron, If I were going to talk with one of your patients, someone who *represents* AIDS, as we head toward 1989, whom might that be? Who might you suggest that wouldn't have been so apt in 1985, but who symbolizes something about AIDS today?

DR. GROSSMAN: [The physician shuffled through folders concealed from Mike's view, like he's making a choice on a juke box.] Would you like to talk about courage? A man fighting Kaposi sarcoma (K.S.) of the lung and who continues to run his business? Someone alive today who couldn't have lasted this long in 1986? He's a publicist for theater, ballet, for rock stars. He's got one of the rarest of the rare AIDS diseases, primary Kaposi sarcoma of the lungs. The difference today is the progress we've made in understanding the disease and in taking aggressive approaches to treatment. And, as you'll see, he has quiet a positive attitude.

MIKE: Yes! Can you arrange an interview?

DR. GROSSMAN: [He was on the telephone in seconds.] Hi Mark. This is Dr. Grossman . . .

Mike Greenly's Interview With Mark Goldstaub
Saturday, September 24, 1988

These are selected comments from the interview I had with Mark Goldstaub:

It is a perfect early autumn afternoon. It is 74 degrees as I approach University Hospital. Upstairs, I find Mark Goldstaub in a hospital bed. He wears dark blue pajamas and black-rimmed sunglasses and he is reclined on bright yellow sheets. In the sunlight pouring in through the windows, I have the momentary image of someone relaxing in a *solarium*. I settle myself into a chair between the windows and his bed, and I notice more details of his condition. The impression of a sunny resort fades away.

He is thin and angular and has a scraggly, light-brown beard. The hair on top of his head is soft and slightly fuzzy, which makes him look fragile, like a baby duck. Tubing and bags of clear liquid hang near the bed. He leans forward in greeting, and I realize that he doesn't really see me. One of his eyes, I learn, is covered with an opaque contact lens, glued in place to put pressure against his cornea.

I begin by asking him for biological information. He has a precise clear voice, a radio announcer's voice, a public speaker's voice. He is 37 years old and he grew up in Maplewood, New Jersey. His college studies in Boston focused on mass communications and theater.

He moved to New York fifteen years ago and got his first job, a public relations position in publishing with Prentice-Hall. He commuted each day from the city to Englewood Cliffs, New Jersey.

In fact, as Mark talked, I began to muse over the similarities between us. My first job was in Englewood Cliffs. Both of us yearned to live in New York, both of us studied communications, began in book publishing, later started our own businesses. He formed Mark Goldstaub Public Relations in 1982, one year before I opened Mike Greenly Marketing. Even our initials, *M.G.*, the color of our hair and our "Jewish" noses make me *think*.

I stare at this man who cannot stare back at me. In one eye he is blind. The other has limited vision. He is talking about his experience in different companies, how he travelled across the country with authors on book tours, how he grew from those travels. I remember, as he talks, my own trips.

"Was it scary," I asked him, "to stop working for others and open your own company?"

"No scarier than life," Mark Goldstaub answered. "There was so much I didn't know. But I'm the sort of person who plunges ahead. I've always been that way. I rolled up my shirt sleeves and did what I had to."

Mark remembered the first pay check he had to write. "My God, I thought, I'm responsible for this person's livelihood!"

Some of Mark's friends had told him it was foolish to open a business and they had tried to discourage him by telling him it wouldn't be easy. Mark said in my interview with him, "But it's never going to be easy. People can always come up with excuses. I didn't want to invent excuses. I wanted *to do it and do it well*."

Since Mark was diagnosed in 1986, he has had two bouts with pneumocystis pneumonia; but, otherwise, he's mostly maintained his health and had not had to alter his daily routine—until now.

Mark explained, "My situation changed drastically in April, after I had this amazing *whammy*, a form of pneumonia that few doctors know much about. It was finally identified as a *K.S.*—exclusively in my lungs. Chemotherapy is the way to treat it, but that can be devastating to the rest of your body. Since chemotherapy last spring, there have been a number of opportunistic infections. There are new dilemmas for me every day."

Mark's company staff fluctuates in number, but typically, there are five people. Lately, he's had assignments publicizing European ballet companies touring America. He continues to captain that work, but now, strictly from a telephone. The hardest adjustment he's had, he says, is *psychological*.

As Mark explained, "Accepting a different work schedule, changing the routine of what work means—that's hard. I'm a typical *Type A* workaholic. I admit it freely. But I've changed my attitude. I don't fit the same patterns I used to . . . I knew that, in finding ways to cope with this disease in my life; I'd have to make major changes. My priorities have shifted. When I started my business, my priority was *let's make a go of this*. Now, my priority is *SURVIVAL*. Frankly, I'm not Superman. I can't continue to pour into my business all the energy required for it to continue at the level we've achieved. I need the energy for myself now. I need the commitment to my own survival, to wellness, to healthfulness. I cannot do both simultaneously. As it is, I'm on the phone as often as I can be. But I'd be dishonest if I said I'm working at the level I used to."

He seems almost apologetic, as though he ought to be working harder. I told him, "Even so, you're still running a business." I wanted to reassure him, and he answered, "Yes!"

Mark also commented about his personal life. "The man I'm in love with, my partner for life, is Edmund. We've been together for seven years, and our relationship has been monogamous for some time, although initially it was *experimental*."

When I asked Mark about his first awareness of AIDS, he explained, "Maybe that was when my friend David called me, about five years ago, and told me he had *K.S.* I remember standing at the kitchen phone, and saying to myself, Oh my God! This is here! This is real! David passed away two years ago. He was 34 or 35. We were close friends.

"I was—you may be surprised, Michael—relieved when I was diagnosed as having AIDS. It meant I could now move to the next phase . . . *saving* myself instead of just *worrying* about whether or not I had it. [Mark paused to *cough*.] If my coughing gets too bad, I'll have to stop talking and catch my breath."

Mark's pajama top was open slightly, and I noticed a bandage on his chest. I asked him about it. He explained, "That's the Hickman catheter." He opened his shirt to show me a tube which ran directly under his skin. It was taped in place. He traced it, under his skin, where it lay like a sleeping worm, but crawling across his chest.

With annoyance at myself, I also noticed I was squeamish as Mark told me how delighted he was with the device. When he needs an intravenous medication, he receives it through the tube. He used to be able to handle the procedure himself, but with his visual problems, he now needs assistance. He explained, "The line underneath," and he pointed to it, "is connected to the subclavian vein, adjacent to my heart. It comes out here, where you see this hub, or what they call the *cap*. You can do anything with it. You can even draw blood!"

I weakly asked, "Is there any pain?"

"I'm not even conscious of it," Mark answered with triumph. "It's an excellent device. You never know how you might use it."

Mark continued his sales pitch for the catheter, as I thought about what an excellent publicist he is. Again, I had the odd awareness of my similarity to him, a man I had never met before. I too, tend to support products I believe in.

Mark volunteered advice to anyone who might be in the hospital with the same verve as his discussion about the catheter. He would tell others, "Get out of bed! You won't have the mobility you're accustomed to having if you sit on your rump for too long. Your muscles will atrophy if they're not being used. You've got to exercise yourself!" He had a perky style when he endorsed anything. Mark had an air of being *chipper* . . . *upbeat* . . . *emphatic!*.

I asked him what he had learned about himself as a result of AIDS, as he was casually chattering on with helpful advice. As I asked that question, I wondered if I was distancing myself from the thin persona in the bed across from me. His head was bobbing slightly as he talked with gusto. I also noticed the black frames of his sunglasses were dotted with specks of yellow, red and blue.

He answered me clearly. "I've learned I am capable of being far more patient than I ever, ever thought. I am capable of receiving love and care and attention and support from a variety of sources that I previously thought I couldn't do. I was too head-strong and narrow-minded and caught up in my own ways."

Again, Mark made me think of myself. I find it easier to give than to accept. What would happen to me, I wondered, if I was in his situation. How would I cope if I had to be dependent? What if I could no longer even connect with my own Hickman catheter? That is what happened to Mark, an energetic independent man. I admire his spunk and equanimity.

Mark continued to talk. "I've been able to enlarge, in a way . . . I can allow today far more than I previously could have . . .

71

things I would once have labeled *right* and *wrong*. Those words aren't a part of my lexicon now."

I asked Mark if he was more tolerant.

He explained, "I don't endow little things with the importance I used to. Life is too short, and little things don't get on my nerves like they used to.

"I'm also far more open to different approaches to wellness and healthfulness than I used to be. Some of my friends were more spiritually advanced than I was when this disease first came my way. Today, I'm more open to different paths that can help me ... to creative visualization ... to other ways of dealing with illness I wasn't aware of before I got sick."

Mark was expecting to go home later that week, and I asked him about his priorities. He told me, "I want to get more well. That's my *first priority*. The long-term is not something I speak of much any more. I want to get well enough, spiritually, to survive this damn thing!

I have never, ever doubted that I would survive this disease. What I have questioned, and what I continue to question, is by what means I'll come by the tools, the techniques, the strategies, the abilities to do this and that. It's never been a question of *if*. It's always been a question of *will I survive?*

"My intention is to survive long enough for things to happen on the medical front—for *medical advancement*. So, what we label now as "fatal" or "terminal" can become "chronic" instead. And, far less severe and simpler to treat. That's what I'm planning on. Then, I could go back and correct some of the damage AIDS has done, like get a corneal transplant to improve my vision."

I told Mark, "You are so *positive*. Have you always been positive?"

He answered, "As far back as I can remember," then he coughed a brutal *hack*, "but without having a name for it.

I suggested, "There must be times you get discouraged."

He admitted, "Yes, of course. Four weeks in a hospital is a long haul. Not being able to see as well as you're accustomed to is a bummer. Talk about *frustrating!* And now that I can't see so well, I have something new to contend with.

72

"But, it's not just me. This condition I have is incredibly difficult on the people I love. What about someone who's had to work all day and then helps you out at night, who has to help you with your catheter. I can't see well enough to handle it. I'm so grateful for the support I get. My parents have been *remarkable*. Edmund has been right there, more than I ever could be, I tell you. My friends too. It's so hard on so many people."

I noticed Mark was taking my questions about himself and turning them into *praise* for others. I asked, "But do you think about the burden on *YOU?* Do you ever feel sorry for *yourself?*

"No," he said. "That doesn't fit." Again, he had a terrible cough before he continued. "I don't focus on getting *in touch* with any burden on myself . . . I focus on having the feelings I need for *coping*, for making what I've determined are all the necessary changes. Feeling sorry for myself wouldn't be *constructive.*

His hands reached out, cautiously, for an alarm clock on his bedside tray. He pulled the clock directly up to his face, just below his glasses. He cocked his head forward to peer at the clock face without letting light from the windows get past his eyeglasses. Then, he felt around to reach a button on the wall.

He said, "Self pity is like guilt. What good does it do?"

From the speaker on the wall, a scratchy voice responded, "YES."

Mark informed the voice, "It's past time for my eye-drops." He was polite, but clear and firm. "Is someone coming around to do that?"

The speaker voice answered, "YES. We're just changing shifts now."

Mark coughed as he said, "Thank you."

I asked him if it hurt when he coughed. He explained, "Sometimes, but not today. The coughing is one of the symptoms of having K.S. on the lungs, as is my shortness of breath. My oncologist attributes it to the breaking up of the lesions inside my lungs. Also, I've lost about 20 pounds of body weight this past year."

Shortly thereafter, a nurse came into the room and administered his eye-drops. She was friendly and pleasant.

"Is the tape back on the catheter?" Mark asked her. She answered, "Yes." I noticed, however, it was never taken off.

After his nurse left the room, I said, "Mark, it's at the end of the time we agreed on. Is there anything you'd like to say directly to anyone who might read this interview?"

He said, "I wish people would acknowledge that AIDS is not always a fatal disease. It's possible to say on top of it. It's conceivable. Yes, it's extremely difficult. It requires probably the biggest commitment one has ever made. But it can be done, and it's important for people to understand that."

As he talked, I could hear the *nattering* in my mind, computing odds, processing statistics, the fact that AIDS—thus far—is mostly *terminal.*

I know how deeply I've come to believe in the *power of attitude, of mental direction," he believes.* I was tugged between my skepticism and the admiration I felt for Mark's approach to illness. Besides, mightn't he be right? Three years ago, when I interviewed medical specialists, the connection between the immune system and psychology was acknowledged as not well understood. Today, there seems to be even more emphasis on that connection, even if not much more is known.

Mark told me, "It's not essential to be passive." He warmly shared that message with the public.

"It's crucial to participate actively in one's own medication. I get information from my doctors to assist my own body in the healing. I ask them questions, which they don't seem to mind.

"I believe the people who ultimately survive are the people who can act that way . . . involved and committed to their wellness . . . and with a support system behind them. I'm so grateful I have the support of loved ones—family, friends, my lover. *I don't know what people do without support. You need more than yourself, alone, as part of the healing process."*

I heard myself *sigh,* as I listened to the tape after my interview with Mark. I wondered about myself, who, in so many ways, am *a loner.*

I had asked Mark, "Are you closer to people, now, actually?"

He answered, "Absolutely! Starting with my lover. We've reached many new depths of closeness. We've enhanced our communications. We don't always discuss pleasant things, of course. It's not always *happiness*. But we're able to talk in ways we never approached before.

"It's the same thing with my parents. The last time they were here, we had a heavy-duty get-together. We had *great communications*, lots of hugging, lots of crying. The three of us came away from the weekend feeling very, very close. The same thing with my brother, Paul."

I began to end the interview with Mark with a question about his hopes for going home again. "In another week, you expect to be home. How will you handle your business, with the challenge of limited vision? Do you have specific thoughts about how you'll handle that?"

He answered, "I just know that it's new, something new to adjust and to incorporate. It will probably be more than I realize now."

He continued. "On one level, it's always hard to go home from the hospital. It's a nuisance to be away from home, but when you go back there, so much of your hospital support is removed. You've been catered to, and while you're glad to be *back on your own turf,* it is not easy.

"Now, yes, I have the further adjustment of going back with limited vision. I'm very conscious of how I've been dealing with it here, and how I've been learning to handle it. I'll just have to do even more of that at home."

It was time to leave. Mark heard me scrape back my chair and stand up. He invited me to telephone him if I needed anything more to add to the story.

He could not see my hand approaching his. His head, his dark glasses and his eyes were not focused directly on me, although I was focused directly on him.

But, his handshake was firm, as was his voice, and I could see sunlight coming from the windows and reflecting from the shiny black lenses over his eyes.

—Michael Greenly is the author of
"*CHRONICLE: The Human Side of AIDS*",
(Irvinton Publishers Inc., 1986.)

CHAPTER EIGHT

Dreams Shattered & Renewed

YES! I WAS ANGRY!
YES! I WAS BITTER!
YES! I DENIED!

I created my own sanctuary of grief and bereavement by the pleasantness of the calming, eternal sea. My son's remains, after cremation, were scattered upon those mysterious waters for eternity.

I look out upon the flowing tide.
My mind wanders past the white-caps of my thoughts.
What is there beyond the sea?
What is out there for me?
Part of me—I'm no longer whole—
rides gently on the waves of Mother Nature.
That missing part is floating in the sea.
God is silent on this lonely beach.

With the loss of a child, the family suffers—not only the heartbreak, but the separation and loss, which is multiplied through the hearts of every family member. The *family unit* can never be the same, so we must learn to take one day at a time.

But it is within reach to *re-create* your family unit. This is a must! From this you will gain strength which you will need for growth. You can go on from there, and you can cope with the *chaos* and *disorder*. Do not allow your family to come apart, and do not go your separate ways.

Think, "We can and we will cope with our losses. We must accept that we cannot change that which has happened. It takes courage to change things which can be changed, but we need to find the wisdom to know the differences."

This does not mean the memory of our lost loved one will vanish. He or she will always be with us. But it does mean *survival*—for the family members who still live and love each other. We will always remember the "good ol' days!" We have many fond memories. For Bernie and I, and Mark's brother, Paul, our departed Mark always wanted us to continue to enjoy life, and we will. Each of us survives for the other and each of us openly expresses our feelings and sense of great loss. Any *catastrophe* cannot be successfully dealt with all at once. Our need to remain strong is monumental. We don't want to lose everything that was important to us before Mark left us.

The knowledge that the three of us were always there when Mark needed us gave us great strength to go on from there.

We did all we could for him when he was alive, and while he struggled through his days of suffering and pain; but, since then, we have transcended that experience, and Mark's love and spirit have guided us to a *new life*.

Before this experience, I could not possibly ever fathom the reality that my world could *explode* in one second and crash into splintered slivers of pain and anguish. Like the snap of a finger, it took only a *flash of time* for my world to fall apart. It happened in the instant that Mark told me, in a quite voice, "*Mom, I have AIDS.*"

The happiness, contentment, and peace which had previously been in my life were instantly torn asunder. The dark foreboding clouds of impending storms suddenly, without warning, destroyed every fiber of my being. The on/off switch of my life was turned *OFF* and I entered a world of seemingly permanent darkness and despair. The psychic torment of losing Mark, our younger son, was overwhelming to Bernie and me.

I kept wondering, over and over, "How can I survive this?" I found, however, that Mark had previously provided me with strength and courage to overcome what he knew would be my *sudden devastation* in life.

During the year and a half Mark struggled for his life, it was his personal strength, courage, determination and constant hope which sustained me, his father, his brother and his lover, Edmund. It was Mark's fortitude and bravery which made me feel so proud he was my son.

Adding to the nightmares of that period of our lives, our older son, Paul, was in the middle of a divorce. Out of the blue, Paul's wife said she still loved him, but no longer wanted to be married to him, after twelve years.

Paul was hurt and distraught. My two devoted sons, loving brothers, were simultaneously struggling with their individual—and each other's—personal, emotional, and psychic pains and tragedies. The trauma that affected all four of us amounted to endless horror.

At that point in time, which was in the fall of 1987, Paul was living in upstate New York. He had accepted a position at Ithaca College as Professor of Music. He was very pleased to become a faculty member at this fine college. He had received his Bachelor of Music at Ithaca and had very fond memories of his four years there before his graduation.

His appointment to the faculty there turned out to be a blessing, and the rest of our family was grateful for the fortunate timing. For Paul, the change of environment was positive for his morale, and it helped him achieve the proper balance of thoughts and feelings—about his pending divorce, his intimate family, and himself.

Soon after his achievement at Ithaca, I wanted to fly up to be with him. However, Mark's illness, Paul's pending divorce, and the intense parent/child/sibling relationships among us all were so disturbing that I just didn't go. I felt, as Paul's mother,

79

that he was alone and that he must need to talk and ventilate his feelings. I knew that he needed me. I also knew I had Bernie by my side and that Mark had Edmund beside him. But that Paul was alone!

It was November and we were back in Florida. The cold was descending upon Ithaca. I called Paul. He was adamant. "Mom, there is no need for you to fly up here. I'm doing just fine and adjusting to the area. My apartment is very comfortable and homey. I'm happy with it. I've met most of the other faculty. I'm pleased. The work is challenging, but I love it. And, Mom, I'm in with a support group, all divorced or *about to be divorced* men and women. So, don't worry Mom, I'm not alone."

He continued, "And, I heard of an AIDS support group. I'm looking into it. I'll get the help I need. You're needed at home for Dad. You give each other so much moral support. You must preserve your energy for Mark. Please, Mom. I'll be fine. I speak to Mark often and when I can, I'll drop down to New York City for a visit with him. I'm only five hours away. I appreciate what you want to do for me, and I love you for it."

I respected Paul's feelings and did not force the issue.

I replied, "Okay, Son. I get the message. You are such an intelligent young man, you'll come through *A-Okay.* You know where you're going. Your love of your work, your music, your talent, your composing, your teaching are all instruments in helping you cope with these upheavals in your life. All are outlets for your emotions."

I reminded him, "Paul, do you remember when you came home from school, I would always *know* what kind of day you had? If you sat down to practice at the piano and played quietly, I knew your day was calm, but if you banged away at the keys, I knew you had a rough day."

We both laughed on the telephone.

"Yup, Mom. You always knew. I do the same thing here. It's a good thing my office is soundproof."

With these happy thoughts, we said our goodbyes. Bernie was on the extension line.

Within a year, Paul's divorce was finalized, amicably. What a welcome relief!

Mark and Paul visited with Bernie and me during the December 1987 holidays. It was the first time in years just the four of us had been together. Edmund had to work and could not get away to join us. Nevertheless, the rest of us had a grand time, a quiet restful week. Just being together was great for us. We talked about everything under the sun. We laughed, we joked, we reminisced and the boys teased each other.

I thought Mark looked well, happy and chipper, and that Paul was adjusting well to his single status. Our sons' lives were back to a semblance of *normalcy*. This was the best medicine for Bernie and me. We played the part of the *happy clowns*, while wearing our *masks of humor*. Were Paul and Mark also acting out their roles?

We all went to the beach, took walks in the surf, ran in and out of the water and splashed each other. We had a picnic and we sat far out on the jetty where we laughed heartily as waves broke against the rocks and sprayed us and dampened our lunch.

The week flew by too fast. We drove Mark to the airport on December 30th. He was going home to spend New Year's Eve with Edmund. As we kissed, hugged and cried, just before he boarded the plane, he turned to me and said, "Happy New Year, Mom! 1988 will be the best year of our lives. You'll see! It'll be the year of *optimism* and *new discoveries*." I thought again of him as the eternal optimist, as I agreed.

Bernie and I were grateful to have Paul stay for another couple of days.

We suffered the natural, acceptable *letdown*, once our children's visit ended, and we questioned ourselves. *How long would Mark remain well?* We hoped his condition would go into remission. Sometimes this happens. I thought, "Please God!"

With time, my "letdown syndrome" subsided and Bernie and I went on with our lives, although with trepidation.

I was slowly making progress as a result of my counseling. I often had setbacks. I knew I had to fight the depression and beat it, for Mark, Paul, and Bernie. They needed me. Marks's *optimism* was the magic factor in my fighting against and beating depression.

Mark developed a *cough* shortly after he returned to New York from Florida. He assured me it was nothing to be concerned about. He said he was working and functioning fine and that his doctor was keeping a check on it.

Our usual routine had been to leave the hot Florida weather at the end of May and spend June, July and August in the cooler atmosphere of New Jersey, where we maintained our apartment year-round.

All through January, February, and into March, I was "holding my own" fairly well. Conversations with Mark always left me on the uphill. But, from one call to another, there was a constant gnawing in the pit of my stomach. I always had to hear his voice, his contagious optimism, to maintain my high level of hope and to dispel my despair. Toward the end of March, I said to Bernie, "I have this terrible need to see Mark. We have nothing to hold us here until June and our New Jersey apartment is waiting on us."

Was it *motherly intuition*? I didn't know, but I felt we needed to go up north. I suggested to Bernie, "Suppose we leave here by April first instead of waiting until June? We'll have that extra couple of months to visit with Mark and Edmund. Maybe we'll take a trip up to Ithaca to visit with Paul, as well."

Bernie was as anxious as I was to leave Florida, so we did on April First, 1988. If there really is such a thing as being at the *right place at the right time*, it most assuredly applied to Bernie and me. Shortly after we arrived in Jersey, Mark's cough was diagnosed as being caused by Kaposi sarcoma (K.S.), which involves cancerous lesions to the lungs. A rarity, at that time, it was thought that K.S. developed on the outer skin layers. Doctors have since learned differently.

Mark was, consequently, admitted to New York University Medical Center for more tests and experiments. The next assault on his body was *chemotherapy*.

Thus, again, we started our trek into New York City. At the hospital, Mark questioned the doctors incessantly. He insisted upon knowing exactly what to expect from his treatments, the after effects, side effects and everything.

Mark suggested to me, "Mom, I think you and Dad shouldn't come to visit me immediately after my first "chemo" treatments. It'll take me a couple of days to get over the side affects. I don't know exactly what they'll do, but I'm sure I'll have some *discomfort*. Edmund will keep in touch with you. Okay?"

Did we have a choice? As hard as it was for me, a mother, not to be constantly at the side of my terminally ill son, I acquiesced to his wishes. I danced to his music to relieve him of unneeded stress, as he, in his heart, had tried to spare his family from suffering with him. On the horns of this dilemma, we prayed that Mark's extraordinary determination would pull him through his newest crisis.

He did suffer the expected side effects and would not permit us to see him until two or three days after each treatment, when he was more comfortable and in less pain. He rationalized that, if he had his chemotherapy administered early in the week, by the end of the week he would be in better spirits, and the effects would dissipate somewhat. That would, by his reasoning, be a good time for us to visit. So, we traveled to the hospital only on Saturdays and Sundays.

The first time we saw him after his second treatment, Bernie and I met Mark and Edmund in the solarium, near the elevator. As Bernie stepped out of the elevator, we first saw Edmund pushing a wheelchair towards us. Then we realized the frail man with thinning hair sitting in the wheelchair was our son, Mark.

Seeing my handsome, strong, well-built son in that condition shocked me so that I felt weakness in my knees. My heart was pounding and there was tightness in every fiber of my being. I had to hold on to the wall to keep from collapsing. The unspoken fear and sorrow overwhelmed me. I could not allow my son to know what I was feeling at that moment. I can only try to recall and remember what *inner force* guided me; but I willed myself to hide my pain and, instantly, functioned in a normal manner.

We ran over to Mark and we all exchanged greetings, kisses and hugs. Mark suggested we find seats at the far end of the solarium, overlooking the water. He was wearing dungarees, a plaid sport shirt, and bedroom slippers which we had brought to him as a gift on another occasion.

The four of us sat and talked. Mark joked about his *thinning hair*. At that point, I asked about his treatments and his progress and, of course, his prognosis. I just blurted out every-thing that was eating me up inside. My nerves were fraying to the point of losing control, but, my questioning was done with an unexplained calmness. Mark, being so perceptive, sensed what I was experiencing, and just as calmly as I asked him questions, he questioned me.

Then he described what chemotherapy was, what it was supposed to accomplish, what his feelings were about receiving the treatments, and whether it was the *right* or *wrong* treatment.

All the gray areas! Something better than nothing, I thought. Listening to him speak with such assurance did not help me that day as it had in the past. I excused myself in search of a restroom.

I made it inside just in time to regurgitate. While I was alone inside the privacy of that room, I put my head down between my knees to keep from passing out. I stayed in the restroom longer than the average time. Before going out, I splashed cold water over my face a number of times. I checked my lipstick and hair, composed myself, then returned to my family.

I knew I would be questioned. And I lied when Bernie asked, "Syl, dear, are you okay? What took you so long?"

I told him, "Yes, I'm fine. I met a woman whose husband is here and we talked. That's all."

It wasn't until Bernie and I were comfortably at home that evening that I told Bernie what really happened. He had ex-perienced the same sensations I had, but controlled himself better than I.

After a number of chemotherapy treatments and many tests, Mark's doctor had him discharged from the hospital. The doctor's estimated period for the treatments was three to six months, as an out-patient. That meant until the end of June or July, or perhaps, August.

Mark's reaction to chemotherapy became less and less noticeable. At first we visited him only when he was strong enough to handle our being with him, but I telephoned him every morning and night. There came a time that he felt annoyed at me for paying so much attention. The strain and stress of the debilitating condition, and the unending stress he knew Bernie and I were suffering, were too much for Mark to cope with at the time.

But I had this need to speak with him every day to *maintain my sanity*.

Then one evening Edmund telephoned me to say, "Sylvia, please, I hope you understand that Mark loves you. We all love you, but I must ask that you do not continue to call him so often. Twice a day is putting too much stress on him. He understands your needs, but he cannot handle and does not need this extra pressure at this time.

"Mark asked me to call and explain this to you. He could not handle telling you himself. I hope you understand. You know what I'm saying? We must do this for Mark."

I answered, "Yes, Edmund, I understand. You are 100 percent correct. I should have realized. I know Mark is right, and you are right in calling me. Don't be upset. I'll talk to him and let him know I understand."

Edmund lovingly advised, "Call him twice a week. We'll call you and arrange for you and Bernie to visit with him when he's comfortable. I'll call you as often as I can, even from my office. I promise. We all have his welfare uppermost in our minds and hearts. He loves you and Bernie so much it hurts him to see you suffer. He knows what you're going though. Believe me! Mark wouldn't do anything to hurt either of you in a million years. He's sleeping right now, so he doesn't know I'm calling you."

I responded, "Edmund, dear, I love you. You are such a devoted, loving compassionate young man. Mark is lucky to have you, so please, thank you for calling. Tell Mark you spoke with me. No problem. We love you both. I'll wait until I hear from you. Put your mind at rest and have a good night. All our love. Bye."

A few nights later, I received a call from Paul. He said, "Mom, I've *got to talk to you*. I hope you'll understand. I know you'll understand. I had a long talk with Mark the other night.

Please, Mom, he told me you call him too often with questions that he can't handle. He understands *why*, but he wishes you wouldn't call him so much. He doesn't have the answers for you and it stresses him not to be able to comfort you."

Paul paused before proposing, "I have an idea! Why don't you and Dad come up here to Ithaca for a few weeks? I have the room, and we can go sightseeing. It is so beautiful here this time of year. I know you want to be close to Mark, but think about it. I know you and Dad will love it here! Come on! Don't even think about it. Just come. The change will be good for both of you and it will please me, Mark, and Edmund."

I told Paul, "I had a long talk with Edmund, and I know what you're trying to do. I understand. Dad and I are lucky to have such caring children—you, Mark, and Edmund. Okay! I'll talk to Dad and get back to you."

That night, in the summer of 1988, Bernie and I talked. He also tried to convince me it would be best if we were away from Mark and from New York. Reluctantly, I agreed.

We drove up to Ithaca for part of the summer. We spoke to Mark and Edmund often, but when they called us. I resisted calling them.

The beauty of Ithaca and the constant activities Paul involved us in were great medicine for me. My heart, emotions and thoughts were constantly with Mark, however.

During the summer, Mark would have his doctor stop the chemotherapy for a week or two at a time. Mark's body dictated the need for a reprieve from that *questionable* treatment.

All the time he was receiving chemotherapy, Mark was gallantly carrying on his business from his home in New York.

I often wondered that, perhaps, if Mark had not given so much of himself to his business, but had left more of it up to his most capable staff, he might have had more energy to devote to his recovery. But that was not my son. Mark gave *all* of himself. He loved his work. He loved the challenges. He met the challenge. The only challenge he lost was to AIDS—a challenge that was out of his control.

After Bernie and I returned to New Jersey in mid-August, we were hit with another *whammy*. Mark's left eye became a problem. The ophthalmologist discovered one of Mark's retinas was damaged. Mark was consequently required to see an ophthalmology specialist who was qualified to treat AIDS patients. He went in for treatments every other day.

At that time, AIDS treatments of any sort were almost a *hit or miss* situation. Even the ophthalmologist's treatments were *uncertain.*

Mark's business required constant reading about theatrical happenings. Newspapers had been very important to him and his company, so we were very concerned about his eyesight and ability to read.

Our plans were to return to Florida around the middle of September, but after Mark's eyesight crises developed, I refused to leave New Jersey.

Mark had vision in one eye, but only shadow perception in the damaged eye. He informed me that arrangements had been made for some of his buddies, People With AIDS (PWA), to help each other during times of need. There was always someone available to assist when needed. Mark and Edmund called on a buddy to take Mark to the eye specialist for appointments. Even though he had the sight in his good eye, it was advisable not to travel alone.

I was about to suggest, "Son, Dad and I can take you anytime," but I suddenly remembered our conversation with Edmund, so I backed off.

Early in the morning after Labor Day, I received a call from Mark. "I'm supposed to go to the doctor for an exam today and my buddy is sick," he explained. "No one is available on short notice, and Edmund has to be out of town on business. Will you and Dad please come and take me?"

I was so thrilled he asked us. We dropped everything and hoped we could make the bus schedule. Neither Bernie or I trusted our emotions that day to drive into New York City.

We boarded the bus near home, which took us to the bus terminal in New York City. From there, we took a cab to Mark's apartment in East Village. From there, we all traveled to the doctor's office on Lexington Avenue.

In the waiting room, Bernie and I patiently waited for Mark to come out of the examining room. When he did, he gave us *good news!* His eye had shown some improvement.

In the cab, on the way home, Mark asked, "How would you two like to stop off for a cup of coffee in the little coffee shop near my apartment?" We told him yes!

Bernie and I were aglow when Mark picked up a newspaper from the rack outside the shop and turned to the theatrical pages. He was testing his eye to judge what improvements he had in his vision.

The eye, through still blurred in appearance, showed more clarity. Again, Bernie and I were elated that our "Champ" was *beating the odds*.

As we left the coffee shop, Mark held his head high, with dignity, and proceeded to walk without assistance to his apartment.

I thought, NO! My dear son is not going blind! He will again see the faces of Mother Nature, which he so loves.

To this day, and forever, I will never forget hearing Mark tell Bernie and me, on that day after Labor Day, "I love you both! Be happy! Don't worry! Keep on dancing, no matter how hard it gets. I overcame all the other damn infections, and I'll do the same with this eye problem."

About ten days later, his right eye became infected. At that point his loss of vision was near total, and there had been just a smidgen of improvement in his left eye.

The consensus of his doctors was that it would be to Mark's advantage to enter the hospital. An AIDS specialist from Atlanta was a staff member there and was willing to put Mark on an experimental eye program. Mark consented to this, and we canceled our plans to return to Florida in September. That put our lives on hold.

After his new program began, Mark received both chemotherapy and eye medications. After days of consultation, his doctors decided that Mark's condition required that either he continue with chemotherapy for K.S. or take the experimental drugs for his eyes. His K.S. was slowly improving, but the combinations of the different drugs for different treatments were interfering with each other.

Mark's decision was to stop chemotherapy for a period of time. It was, at that time, affecting his legs. Thus, he continued with the experimental eye treatments.

This colossal decision was mind-boggling for him to make, and he did not tell us of the need for such a choice until after it was made.

His stay in the hospital was left "in the lap of God." No attempt was made by anyone to predict or approximate the outcome of the *experiment*. His doctor saw him every day, at the same time of day. Administration of the drug had to be precise, with no deviation of time!

One day we arrived at the hospital a bit earlier than scheduled. Mark was just walking out of the examination room. I say "walking," but it was actually more like "flying" or "floating through space." His doctor had just given him a most encouraging report. One eye had leveled off. It had not gotten any worse for a period of time, and the other eye showed a definite improvement.

Mark grabbed us, danced around the room and sang, "I love you all. I love you! I love you! I love my body! I'm getting better! I see! I See! I SEE!"

His reaction was electrifying. He finally calmed down. He immediately called Edmund to give him the *good news*. "I want to call Paul and tell him too!" he joyfully told Edmund.

A temporary "*seventh heaven*" for all of us! An *ecstasy of delight.*

I walked to the foyer to get a glass of water and there, quite unexpectedly, encountered Mark Jollie, whom I have called a "*Saint.*" That remarkable young man had been our tower of strength ever since we first talked to him in a doctor's office, almost a year previously. He has always been there for us, ever since.

The moment he looked at me, he said, "Sylvia! Mark's having a good day, isn't he?" He's given you *good news* hasn't he?"

I asked him, as I smiled, "How did you know? You haven't seen him today?"

Mark answered, "My dear Sylvia, all I have to do is look into your eyes and your face. You are all glowing! I haven't seen this look on your face for many months."

IV. HUMANITY

Mark Neil Goldstaub

**THE HUMAN RACE,
HUMANKIND,
THE FACT OR QUALITY OF
 BEING HUMANE:
KINDNESS,
MERCY,
SYMPATHY.**

**THE LIFE GOODNESS OF HEART
GIVES TO EACH OTHER!**

**TAKE A GIGANTIC LEAP
FOR ALL HUMANITY!**

CHAPTER NINE

One Love, One Heart, One Soul

Needless to say, all of us were on *Cloud 9* after we learned of the remarkable improvement of Mark's eye problem. His doctors were astounded. The K.S. also showed signs of going into remission . . . REMISSION! What a wonderful word!

Remission would give him time, even though it would be temporary. We all knew it could be only temporary, but nevertheless, it meant *time.*

Perhaps it could be permanent, we thought. Who could say? Once again, my son's extraordinary will and perseverance came to the forefront. Another dilemma had "hit the dust," and Mark was "The Champ" again, winner over the dilemmas of AIDS.

He did, however, have to continue with eye treatments, but these could be administered at home by a professional nurse. Pauline Perez was assigned to Mark's case. This extraordinary woman became his "adopted grandmother." She and he shared fun moments together, or, as she called it, "personal moments."

"Sylvia," she explained, "Mark often talked for hours at a time about his growing-up years—his mostly good, but sometimes unhappy days as a child. He often spoke of his love of his family. He remembered talking to your mother, his grandmother, about her life in the old country, in Russia, as a little girl. He had great times with all of you, his family.

"He loved going ice skating, playing tennis, going on car trips and the long Sunday drives. He remembers the fun of stopping off for ice cream cones on those rides, and teasing his dad about not liking ice cream but having a cup of coffee instead."

I could remember Mark saying, "Hey Dad! How could anyone not like ice cream?"

Pauline continued. "He was happy telling me about all these happenings with his family."

"Yes," I agreed. "We had great times and we thought they'd never end."

I thanked Pauline and added, "You will always hold a special place in my heart. You gave my son happiness the last days of his life. He never stopped telling me how he appreciated your being with him. He truly loved you."

I functioned on an even level for the first time in months, mentally, physically and emotionally.

With all of us "floating on air," Mark settled back at his apartment, in high spirits. Bernie and I returned to Florida in October. The word *REMISSION* was indelibly imprinted upon my brain.

Between calls, instead of writing, we made tapes of our daily happenings. Mark so enjoyed the lengthy descriptions of places, people, and events in our lives. He laughed hysterically at the off color jokes his Dad told him on the tapes.

"Dad, I play them over and over," Mark amusingly said. He appreciated the tapes of books by his favorite author, which we also sent him.

As his eyes improved, and he was able to recognize the alphabet and numbers, I sent him *affirmations*—positive statements directed to his inner mind, which helped create positive state of being or action. Changes began immediately.

Mark Goldstaub and Tommy Tune.

I printed them on large yellow legal size sheets. I made each letter large enough and thick with a black marking pen. I taped each page to the bottom of the other, making a list about five feet in length. Then, when he received it, Edmund mounted in on the wall opposite Mark's bed.

Mark told me, "Mom, I'm ecstatic! I can read most of it. Each day, I see the letters more clearly." They read as follows:

1. I AM THE I AM SINCE TIME BEGAN I AM.
2. EVERY DAY IN EVERY WAY I AM
GETTING BETTER-BETTER-BETTER.
3. THE ETERNAL LIGHT FLOWS THROUGH ME, IN ME AND PROTECTS ME.
4. WHEN I GO INTO MY SILENCE I FIND MY INNER PEACE.
5. LOVE FLOWS IN ME, TO ME, THROUGH ME AND FROM ME IN EVERYONE I MEET.
6. WHAT I BELIEVE TO BE - WILL BE.
7. I FOLLOW MY PATH AND I WALK AT MY OWN PACE.
8. TODAY I AM RELAXED!

Over time, I continued to send him additional affirmations. We continued to give Mark his personal space, but visited whenever he asked, "How about you guys coming up to visit with me next week?"

We would hastily and happily reply, "Son, we are on our way." Those joyous visits took place every few weeks.

For the three to four days of each visit, we stayed at a nearby hotel rather than disturb Mark's routine. As much as he wanted us to stay at his place, he understood our logic.

Paul often arranged his schedule to coordinate his visits with ours, so that we all had quality family time together. Mark, Edmund, Pauline, Paul, Bernie and I were a happy family.

Those memories added to so many other precious memories. Memories of happy, proud occasions that we shared with our sons, Mark, Paul, and yes, Edmund.

Mark represented the Broadway show, "*A Day in Hollywood—A Night in the Ukraine,*" at the Royale Theatre on 45th Street, west of Broadway. During the show, Pricilla Lopez did an impersonation of Groucho Marx, a routine that was a show stopper. Tommy Tune was the choreographer. The show won the "*Best Musical of the Year 1980*" award, and was the funniest show to hit broadway in years.

June 17th was Bernie's and my thirty-fifth wedding anniversary, and Mark had arranged for us and some friends to attend the show that night. Afterward, he surprised us with an after-theatre late supper in Sardi's Restaurant—at the best table in the house.

He sent the following singing telegram to us at Sardi's:

TO MOM AND DAD
HERE'S A SONG TO CELEBRATE
ON YOUR ANNIVERSARY.
IT'S A SLIGHTLY SENTIMENTAL TUNE
BUT I HOPE THAT YOU'LL AGREE
IT EMBODIES ALL THE LOVE YOU SHARED
THE JOY THAT'S THERE FOR ALL TO SEE.

ONE LIFE ONE HEART ONE SOUL
ONE EVERLASTING SERENADE

YEARS PASS AND RECEDE
LIFE PAYS NO HEED
YOUR LOVE HAS BLOSSOMED IN SPRING
TOUCHING EVERYTHING
TURNING ROUND AND ROUND
YEARNING FOR THE SOUND OF THE HARMONY
IT'S YOUR DESTINY TO LIVE YOUR LIFE
IN LOVE AS ONE

SO COUNT YOURSELVES BLESSED
CAUSE YOU'VE GOT EACH OTHER
IN A WORLD FULL OF LONELINESS AND FEAR
YOU HAVE SAID YES TO LIFE
AND MUST ALWAYS HOLD IT DEAR
ONE LOVE ONE HEART ONE SOUL
ONE SERENADE THROUGHOUT THE YEARS.

LOVE,
YOUR SON MARK

We were so proud of him and thankful he found his successful career. We were thankful we all were together to share his success and happiness.

Through our son's career, we had many opportunities to meet world-renowned performers. He knew we got a kick out of speaking with these celebrities. He made it a point to take us backstage to their dressing rooms after performances.

Mark represented the Metropolitan Opera House at Lincoln Center. It was a thrill to shake the hand of Rudolph Nureyev after his performance in *Swan Lake*. While waiting for the ballet to start, Mark introduced me to Mr. Nureyev's body guard, a large-built, elegant, gallant gentleman. He kissed my hand and was so very gracious, I felt as though I were the Queen of England. Mark always had a seat available at the Metropolitan Opera for his composer, conductor, brother Paul.

When we congratulated Hershel Bernardi, in his dressing room at Lincoln Center after his brilliant performance in "*Fiddler on the Roof,*" he said to Bernie, "Don't congratulate me. I thank your son. He deserves all the credit. He did such a great public relations job. If not for him, I wouldn't be here. You should be very proud of him. He is a fine young man."

Bernie happily responded, "We are very proud. I want to thank you for your kind words. They're very deeply appreciated."

April 19, 1984, was Opening Night for Shirley MacLaine on Broadway. Mark Goldstaub Public Relations was her East Coast representative. By special invitation, we were invited to attend the show and dinner and dancing at Regine's afterward.

Bernie and I arrived in New York a few hours early, checked in at our hotel, and immediately went from there to Mark's office to say hello.

The office was a bee hive of shouts, laughter, movement and sound. Everyone was busy getting set for Shirley's opening night. After our hugs and kisses, Mark put Bernie and me to work. We sat on the floor and prepared programs for opening night. Hours later, exhausted, but having enjoyed every minute, we all went out to dinner. The treat was on Mark Goldstaub.

After Shirley's great performance, we were escorted to Regine's. Surrounded by hundreds of the rich and famous from

Mark Goldstaub Fulfilled Shirley MacLaine's Dream to Ride An Elephant!

all walks of life, we were all asked to be seated. Miss MacLaine was arriving. The drums rolled and a gust of applause and a standing ovation greeted her. Mark was holding her hand as they entered.

Shirley had just won an Academy Award for her performance in *Terms of Endearment*. We were proud and beaming as we applauded. As Mark and Shirley walked by our table, Marked stopped a moment and introduced us to Shirley.

Shirley MacLaine and Mark shared the same birthdate. Being an excellent publicist, he learned she had a great desire to ride an elephant, one of the few things she had not accomplished. He immediately arranged to surprise her for her birthday by having an elephant greet her at the stage door when she arrived for rehearsal on April 24th.

She could not have been more thrilled. She rode the elephant down Broadway with all branches of the media following. The story and pictures all made the front pages. It was a fantastic public relations feat, and Mark received many accolades from his fellow PR colleagues. He was very proud of himself and so were we.

Regis, Sylvia and Bernie Goldstaub.

Exciting, funny memories took place at the Westbury Music Fair in Long Island, one of Mark's favorite and long-standing accounts.

Henry Youngman was celebrating his 80th birthday, and as Mark started to introduce Bernie and me to Mr. Youngman backstage, Bernie shook the comedian's hand, turned to me and threw Henny Youngman his famous line, "Take my wife, please!"

Before Mr. Youngman could retort, Mark yelled out, "No! Don't take her! She's my mother. I need her!"

Everyone roared with laughter. Henny replied, "This is the first time I could remember someone beating me to a retort." He was a great sport about it.

On our 40th anniversary, our children, Paul and his wife, Mark and Edmund, secretly planned a week-long surprise celebration for us. They arranged for our stay at a posh hotel in New York City, and every day and night there was a very special surprise program. We never knew from one day to the next what was in store for us.

We appeared on a National TV talk show, where they publicly announced our 40th anniversary. We saw the latest Broadway shows, operas, ballets and movies. One evening we went to a Mets ball game, for old times sake. And, the Mets won!

Bernie, Edmund, Sylvia and Mark.

101

We had dinners at New York's most prominent night clubs. The *piece de resistance* was the last night of celebration. We all went to the Westbury Music Fair to see Tom Bosley and his wife perform in *Fiorello*. The cast was gathered in his dressing room. When I walked in with Bernie, Paul, his wife, Mark and Edmund, they all yelled "Surprise and congratulations!"

Tom Bosley opened a bottle of champagne, made a special toast, and we all drank to the celebration of our anniversary.

One of the men in the room remarked, "I have been married three times, and all three marriages don't add up to 40 years. How do you do it?" The room was filled with joy, laughter, and lots of kidding.

Our surprise week of celebration ended up in a splendid joyous spirit. Most importantly, the six of us—our family—could be together, love and care. It was an incredible week, never to be forgotten.

The last famous person Mark introduced his family to was the magnificent Mary Martin, a most talented leading lady of the theater. We met her in Florida in January of 1987, during a visit from Mark and Paul. Edmund did not visit that time because of work in New York.

Mary Martin was performing in *Legends* at the Royal Poinciana Playhouse in Palm Beach. Mark had been her publicist for the *Tribute to Mary Martin*. They grew very fond of each other. Mark called the office of the Playhouse, and had no trouble getting us seats.

I was a mother bursting with thrilling pride! I was so proud when the lovely Mary Martin opened the door to her dressing room, after the show, and saw my son, hugging and kissing him, she said, "Mark, I love you and I miss you." He introduced Mary to Bernie, Paul, and me. She invited us to sit and talk with her.

I told her how much I had enjoyed her performances over the years. We had seen her on Broadway, from the best seats in the house, the first time she sang "My Hear Belongs to Da-Da-Daddy." She mesmerized the audience that night, and has continued to do so. She thanked me with a bright sparkle to her dancing eyes and a radiant smile on her famous face, before announcing, "I just received a call from my son Larry. He has become a grandfather, and I am so very, very excited and thrilled to be a great-grandmother!"

Mary cheerfully added, "And, they named the little girl after me! I can't wait to see her!" We offered our best wishes and good luck.

As we were leaving, Mark asked if she would please pose for a picture with me. Mary was most gracious and charming. "Take two or three shots in the event one doesn't come out. Make sure your mom has a good picture."

Mary Martin and Sylvia Goldstaub at Poinciana Playhouse.

Later, Mark picked out the best one, had it framed and gave it to me. It hangs on the wall in my bedroom. I'll always treasure it.

Imprinted in my mind and in my heart are encores of these treasured memories of my son over the few healthy, happy, productive years since he was born.

Bernie, myself and son, Paul, have added stature, grace and meaning to our lives and we were able to give Mark Unconditional Love during his final hours of need. We were there for him and he knew it! As Mark said, "We were *one love, one heart, one soul!*

If we had allowed ourselves to become estranged, or if we had left Mark to live his life apart from us, we would live the rest of our lives with regret, guilt and terrible sadness in our hearts.

My mind recalls Matt's life of estrangement, perpetuated by his mother. She separated herself from her son's life for 25 years. How sad for her. After compassionate, supportive Matt passed away in August 1990, we attended his memorial services. A few days later, his mother called me.

"Sylvia," she confessed, "I had to call you to thank you for Matt and for myself. Shortly before Matt died, he told me all about you and the relationship your family shared with your son Mark. I'm sorry to hear about your loss, and I have such a heavy heart.

"You and your husband gave my son, initially a complete stranger to you, the love, acceptance and compassion I wasn't there to give him. My ignorance robbed me of my son.

"I have 25 years of my life without a memory of my fine, dear son. I was so wrong. Why do we humans do these things to ourselves? It is so true. We are our own worst enemies!

"Until the day I die," Matt's mother said, with tears in her eyes, "I'll always regret and feel terrible guilt for the negative attitude I took with Matt. I'll never forgive myself. I learned, but too late."

Paul, Bernie, Mark and Sylvia.

CHAPTER TEN

From Newborn to Business Man

I was due to give birth on or about March 18, 1951. It was unusual for a delivery to be approximately six weeks late. Even in the womb, our son Mark had a "mind of his own." He would enter this world when he was ready—not because of a miscalculation of dates.

I was the only woman in the hospital who was walking around with a baby still in her belly on a floor with mothers who had already given birth. The hospital's policy, in those days, was that the expectant mother would remain on the Delivery Floor until she gave birth. After the baby arrived, she was placed in a room on another floor, with other mothers and their babies.

At home, I had shown signs of delivering on Monday night, April 23rd, between 9:30 and 10:00 p.m. I telephoned Dr. Silverman and explained my timing to him. Bernie, to this day, had "complained" that he had to miss the ending of a *Playhouse 90* television program to follow the doctor's orders: "Go to the hospital immediately!"

As it happened, however, there was no *emergency*. It was a "false alarm." The doctor next advised, "Go home and wait it out. You're not quite ready. Maybe . . . in the morning, or perhaps, another 24 hours. We don't know," he explained.

He added, "The apple doesn't fall from the tree until it is ready."

Dr. Silverman tried to comfort me as I explained, "No way! Doctor, if you remember my first delivery, I was rushed back and fourth to the hospital twice with "false alarms." This time, I'll just stay here and wait—especially since I'm 'supposedly six weeks late already'." I was so insistent that Dr. Silverman had me assigned to a room to wait it out on the post-delivery floor.

On Tuesday, April 24, 1951, at 6:30 p.m., after I delivered Mark, Dr. Silverman told me, "Sylvia, you are going to make another *briss* (circumcision). You have given birth to a fine, complete baby boy! All is OKAY. He weighs 8 pounds, 9 ounces and he's 20 inches tall. *Mozel Tov!*" So my obstetrician announced at Mark's birth.

My newborn son was of medium complexion, had beautiful, big, brown eyes, a lot of black hair, strong fingers, and "perpetual motion."

Dr. Silverman jokingly said to me, "Sylvia, for a small gal, you sure knock out big babies!"

He had delivered our first son, Paul Robert, three years and eight months before. Paul weighed in at 8 pounds, 15 ounces.

Dr. Silverman also said, "I hope you're not disappointed you didn't have a girl. You'll probably make a girl next time."

I said, "No way, Dr. Silverman! I'm not at all disappointed. Thank God, my baby finally arrived and we both came through healthily. As a matter of fact," I continued, "I'm happy I have another boy. For some reason or other, I'm partial to little boys."

Then, I asked, "Do you want to hear a funny story about myself and little boys?" I didn't wait for him to answer, knowing he had a wonderful sense of humor. He was always telling jokes and ready for a laugh, so I proceeded.

"As I child, I never played with girls. I can't remember owning a doll. I could never understand little girls who played with dolls, which I viewed as *dull, spiritless, silent objects.*

"I preferred alive and active playmates, and boys' activities—marbles, climbing trees, playing ball, actions, skills.

You name it, I did it. Running down the street hitting a hoop from a wooden barrel with a stick, for example. I was accepted by all the male kids.

"With six children and little income, my father drove a truck for a dry cleaning company. There wasn't much money to spare for the barber, so my mother was our barber. In the early 1920s, the "boyish bob" was the hair style of the day.

"Looking like a boy, I fit right in with the neighborhood boys. I wore my older sister's hand-me-down pants instead of dresses when I went out to play. Due to my athletic prowess, I was nicknamed "Tomboy" by my family. This name stuck with me for many years."

"So, what happened next?" Dr. Silverman wanted to know.

I continued. "Years later, my mother related a story to me about the time I was about four or five years old, and we were invited to a "dress up" family affair. I was wearing a dress, and we were leaving the house. One of the neighbors saw us and asked my mother, 'Why is *Tomboy* wearing a dress?'"

My mother simply stated, "Girls *do* wear dresses!"

The neighbor blurted, "Well, I never knew *Tomboy* was a girl."

I further explained to Dr. Silverman, "With my ability to keep up with my male playmates, my boyish haircut, and the nickname "Tomboy," I often wondered, over the years, if the kids I played with knew I was a *girl*."

We both had a hearty laugh. Then I added, "That's why I prefer *little boys*. I don't think I would know what to do with a *baby girl*."

Dr. Silverman laughed again. Then I said, "Thanks for listening and for doing such a grand job! Good luck on your future deliveries. I don't expect you'll see me again, after my final check-up.

"Bernie and I don't plan to have any more children. Just the four of us, counting little Mark here, we will be very happy and love each other forever!"

Bernie and I named our newborn son *Mark Neil Goldstaub*.

BIRTH ANNOUNCEMENT
Paul Robert Goldstaub
Is Proud and Happy
To Announce
The Birth of His Brother,
MARK NEIL GOLDSTAUB
Born: Tuesday, April 24, 1951 at 6:30 p.m.
Weight: 8 pounds, 5 ounces

Mark was a happy, active, healthy baby, but not the easiest baby to handle. Or perhaps it was that I was unprepared for his aggressive, forceful personality during the infant stage of his life.

He was most definite with his likes and dislikes: his eating habits, sleeping habits, wants, etc. He could not be coaxed into taking any nourishment he did not want. He accepted the food he wanted when he wanted it.

The same routine applied to his sleeping habits, when and for how long he wanted to sleep. I tried to establish the routine of putting him into his crib shortly after the six o'clock evening feeding (if he chose to accept food at that time), hoping he would be set for a full, good night of sleep.

This was not Mark's intention. After about an hour or so of sleep, he would awake and cry until I picked him up.

This went on for weeks and into months. I tried everything in the books to get him to give up the tantrums and sleep through the night.

My pediatrician assured me, "If you do not pick him up, he will eventually take the hint and fall asleep from exhaustion."

Living in close proximity to neighbors whose youngsters were sleeping soundly for hours, I felt it was not fair to them to allow my baby to cry for perhaps hours until the "Sand Man" took hold. It would also keep his brother, Paul, awake.

I braced myself and told our neighbors. I had their sympathy. We all hoped the pediatrician's method would do the trick and that the neighborhood would soon be sleeping peacefully ever after.

Mark, however, had other ideas! He quickly developed a new *technique*. As soon as he realized that crying was going to be ignored, he added a *jumping up and down act* to his repertoire. He did it in the corner of his crib, along with crying, and he had such fortitude! This continued every night for at least an hour before he became exhausted. Finally, I won the battle of sleep. I still wonder, did I really?

His show of independence as an infant was just the forerunner to his forceful character as a grown man. Mark spoke and walked at a very early age. His first word was "brother," for which Paul was very proud. Most children's first words are *da-da* or *ma-ma*. And, before long, he amazed us by starting to speak in full sentences!

His determination was such that when I changed him from diapers to training pants, before he was a year old, he understood this purpose and never soiled a pair of training pants. It made my motherly duties much lighter!

At two years of age, Mark had to have a tonsillectomy. In the days of the early 1950s, tonsillectomies were performed in the hospital and patients were normally discharged the same day.

Mark, however, was bleeding more than usual, and his doctor recommended we leave him at the hospital overnight. We promised Mark we would stay there through the night, unaware, however, that this violated hospital policy.

Once he was asleep, the hospital staff advised us we would have to leave. We left, with a nurse's assurance that if Mark awakened, she would explain why we weren't there. Well, he woke up, we weren't there, and his nurse had neglected to tell him why we weren't there.

When we arrived back at the hospital very early the next morning, Mark was standing in his crib, dressed, waiting for us. He pointed his finger at us and started to cry. His throat was sore from the tonsillectomy, but he managed to exclaim, "You broke your promise! You said you would stay with me!"

This fiery response to our absence was a clear indication of Mark's life-long *sense of fair play*. We still think this led to his successful life and career.

Bernie worked long hours, in those years, and generally left the house before the children got up in the morning. He often returned home after I had put them to bed. It was only on weekends—half-days on Saturdays (sometimes) and Sundays—

that the three males in my life and I spent time with each other. It was not a lot of time, but it always was *quality time!*

Bernie and I always believed *humor is our best friend!* We loved to laugh. We all had a great sense of humor and we often displayed it. For the four of us, it was a life of *laughs, love, kisses and hugs.* That was routine at our home.

At pre-school age, Mark showed a definite love of nature. We lived on the first floor of a two-story garden apartment in Maplewood, New Jersey. It had one bedroom for Bernie and me and a den converted to a bedroom for Paul and Mark. Their room overlooked a small grassy area. Mark proclaimed that area as his tomato garden. He dug up the earth with his bare hands, loving every minute of it, and planted tomato seeds. He checked the progress of his crop from the minute his he opened his eyes every morning.

Our friendly neighbors had great affections for Mark. They enjoyed being with him, sensing his knowledge and laughing at his sense of humor. During summer, at the end of each day, after our sons were asleep, we and our neighbors would gather on the front lawn for an hour or two for rest, relaxation, casual talk and telling jokes. It was our outlet from the tensions of the day.

One of the neighborhood husbands, having watched Mark catering to his tomato garden every morning, suggested we pull a prank on Mark. "Let's sew a big, red-ripe tomato on one of the vines!"

A few of the other husbands, and Bernie, thought that was a fabulous idea, so they did just that!

By flashlight, in the darkness of night, grown men took needles and thread to Mark's sacred garden to sew a fine, red, fat tomato onto a vine. Sneaky? Yes, but they all were very fond of him.

The following morning, they anxiously watched from nearby for Mark's reaction, as he did his morning routine of tending his garden.

Bernie and I were awakened by Mark's loud, proud announcement when he ran back inside from the garden. MOM! DAD! PAUL! I grew a tomato!" He dashed back outside in his pajamas, barefooted, to admire his accomplishment.

However, logic took over as he examined the tomato. He realized that tomatoes that large didn't happen overnight. "Okay," he asked. "Who's the wise guy?"

Our friends confessed, "We're the culprits. Mark, with your sense of humor, we knew you'd enjoy the joke along with us. We almost fooled you, didn't we?"

Mark did appreciate their trick and, over the years, he told about it many, many times. He never minded being the *butt* of a joke.

Along with his love of nature, which grew over the years, Mark's love and understanding of his fellow human beings started to emerge.

During his formative years, his understanding, compassion, interest, determination, perseverance, and assertiveness without being aggressive, were the beginning signs of what was in his future.

Mark was by no means the *ideal* child to rear. As all children get into scraps of every nature, so did he. I was happy to see Mark was growing up in a normal, everyday environment of the times, in our culture, just as most of the other boys in our neighborhood were.

Our garden apartment was on a cul-de-sac. Our neighbors shared our lifestyle. We were basically young-marrieds, all with pre-school children, and a camaraderie existed among us. In some cases, it developed into lifelong friendships among parents and children.

We all loved the privacy of our little corner of the world. Not being a through street, no one had any reason to drive into our cul-de-sac without purpose. We named it our own *Shangri-La.*

All the kids—boys and girls—got along quite well, except for the usual childhood differences. A fight now and then, but nothing of any magnitude. Our front lawn became the "gathering spot."

Mark's companions sought him out. Not only his pre-school buddies, but their parents as well. They enjoyed their "chat sessions" with him.

My women friends, especially, loved the comments from my little "five-year-old charmer." He was always saying such things as, "Mrs. Baker, your hair looks so nice. I like the way it's styled. Mrs. Baker glowed as she responded, "Mark, it's so nice of you to notice. My own kids don't notice me. I just came from the beauty parlor."

Or, Mark might say, "Mrs. Robinson, is that a new dress? It looks so well on you." He, for example, also gave his best wishes to Mrs. Livingston when he told her, "Good luck with your new piano. It looks great where you placed it!"

The women called to tell me how thoughtful and observant Mark was—not only to notice, but to have the ability to express his personal feelings without any prompting or hesitation.

Many times, I received telephone calls from neighbors, asking, for example, "Can Mark come over and play with Ellen? Maybe some of his *personality* will rub off on her."

Or, for another example, "Rick is listening to his records. Could Mark come over and keep him company? He plays so well with other children."

And, *RRRRrrrinnnnngggg, RRRRrrrinnnnnnggg!* "Hello, Syl! This is Ruth. I just came home from marketing and Mark came by to help me with the bundles. He's here with me and we're having a nice conversation. I just wanted you to know where he is. Do you mind? He's such a *delight* to have around."

When Ruth called that day, I couldn't help but laugh. I told her, "Of course it's okay. Thanks for letting me know."

As I replaced the telephone to its resting place that day, I thought about how all of us loved Mark's *charming* character. Everybody loved him and he loved everybody. But, if they had to live 24 hours a day with this forceful kid—I also thought—they'd . . . I wondered what.

But, Mark made our lives lively, jumpy, and he kept us on our toes.

His brother, Paul, had his moments with Mark. Sibling rivalry does exist, but I paid little attention to this, since I grew up in a family of six siblings. I knew that rivalry went along with growing up.

As the years went by, and our two fine sons grew into adulthood, their relationships blossomed into sincere and deep friendships, with great respect and mutual admiration for each other.

As Mark grew up, his mind developed beyond his years. Our neighbors, for example, would often come and seek out Mark, whom they had named the *Counselor*. It was most relaxing and stimulating for them to bring their beach chairs to our front lawn, sit down, relax and discuss many subjects with this knowledgeable, loving, outgoing youngster. Mark certainly had a personality that attracted many people toward him, and they never had to encourage this little boy who always was so vocal.

Mark was next ushered into a new chapter of his life. Advanced as he was, in many ways, when it came time for him to enter kindergarten, he behaved the same as most of the other students. And, the *little boy* in him surfaced.

He, along with at least half his class, refused to go into the classroom unless Mom joined them. His "insecurity", however, did not last long. Within a few days, Mark was anxious and happy to be in school, and he progressed along with his classmates.

Some were his playmates from our "Shangri-La" and, others were new personalities he had to learn to deal with. Also, he was no longer under the "rules and thumb of Mom and Dad only". Now, he was thrown into a new environment among complete strangers and a new teacher, whom he was obliged to obey!

Mark accepted what kindergarten had to offer, and he fell in line with all the requirements of his new experience in life. Most importantly, he learned to make and retain new friends outside the familiar circle of his "home base."

Just as he was so outgoing before kindergarten, Mark did not hesitate to express himself in school.

The school he attended had a separate entrance for the kindergarten class. When the bell *rang,* the upper classes entered the building and filed into their classrooms, but the kindergarten children had to wait outside for the teacher to come to the door and admit them in.

There were two sessions for the youngsters—morning and afternoon. When the second session of the school year began, the groups were reversed. Mark started his school life in the afternoon class. He did not hesitate to express his feelings about fair play in the outer environment. Whether adult or child, rules are rules.

I recall a Parent-Teacher Association (PTA) meeting, which was one of many I attended, when I learned from Mark's teacher about an incident which had taken place a few days before. She also shared her observations of Mark, in class, with me.

I began our meeting with, "Fine! That's why I'm here, to hear about my son." I also was keeping my fingers crossed, wondering what she would tell me that I didn't know about that young character of mine.

The teacher said, "Mrs. Goldstaub, Mark is very bright and articulate for his age. He displays warm and loving qualities toward the other children. They like him and follow his lead. He is very assertive and outspoken.

"He shows leadership tendencies; but I have often asked him to refrain from speaking out, and give other children the opportunity to express themselves. He has obeyed this request, but only to a point. I don't know how he behaves at home, or with his playmates outside school, but I think he ought to control his *desire to take over,* or *lead the pack,* so to speak."

She continued. "One afternoon, about a week ago, the upper grades had gone into class. My children were impatiently waiting for me. I opened the door and gestured for them to enter. Mark was about fifth or sixth in line. The minute he saw me, without a moment's hesitation, he immediately reprimanded me for being late.

"Mrs. Kolberg, we're supposed to be here on time. You're the teacher setting an example for us, so you're supposed to be on time."

"All the other children picked up his cue and responded with, 'Yeah!' as they filed into the room. I felt Mark was completely out of line."

I thanked Mrs. Kolberg very much for giving me her evaluation of Mark. I promised, "I'll speak to him about this."

When I arrived home, and told Bernie about my meeting with Mrs. Kolberg, we had a good laugh over it. Our little free-spirited, five-year-old had the courage of his convictions to speak out when he felt an injustice. The teacher resented this youngster reminding her of the *ground rules.*

Early the next morning, Mark ran into our bedroom. "Mom! Dad! What did Mrs. Kolberg say about me?" Paul was right behind Mark, waiting to hear it all.

"You're a great kid, doing fine and your classmates like you. But, Master Mark Neil Goldstaub, you have a big mouth! Watch your tongue," Bernie told him.

I added, "Mrs. Kolberg told me about what you said to her the day she was late. She is your teacher, and you do have to show her respect, even though you were right."

As Bernie was getting ready to leave for work, he said to our sons, "There are different ways of saying things. Often, it isn't what you say, but *the way you say it.* Being a salesman, I've learned this. *Communication* is the key word."

The boys sat on the bed, thoughtfully listening to their dad.

"Hey guys," I reminded them, "time is a-wasting! It's time for work! Time for school!"

Mark jumped up nonchalantly and said to his dad, "Okay!" Then he ran into the kitchen, yelled out, "What's for breakfast?"

During his grade school and high school years, Mark took part in almost every activity: sports, music (he played clarinet). He became the first clarinetist in the school orchestra, and he was in school plays and on the debating team.

In his junior year of high school, he ran for class president, but lost by one vote. His English teacher consoled him by advising that defeat is good "because you learn from it." That teacher became his dear friend and remained his dear friend until the end. The two of them shared a unique relationship, and Mark and her daughter became close, dear friends as well.

At that point in time, we lived in our home in the same town. The school system was the same. Our sons did not have the trauma of making new friends in a new area. Plus, the school system, at the time, was considered one of the best in the country. We wanted our sons to have the best offered in education.

The boys each had their own room. We all had a place to be alone when we felt so inclined. There was a finished room with a bath on the third floor. Mark and his clique adopted it as their private getaway. It was their own "little corner of the world."

A herd of Mark's friends, boys and girls, would think nothing of bursting through the house, into the kitchen (the light inside our refrigerator never went out!) and upstairs. They thundered around like airplanes taking off. Batten down the hatches!

There were never-ending telephone calls for Mark. He was the gang advisor for any problem, especially to the girls. Mark had the solution!

His standard of ethics and leadership quality became a way of life through grade school days, college days and into his public relations world.

In his junior year of high school, he dated a special girlfriend, Nancy. They became a steady pair. Nancy joined our family for Sunday outings, dinner during the week, movies and rides to the seashore. In turn, Mark spent time with her family. They were *the couple*. The hit of the prom!

I remember one night in particular. Mark asked me, "Mom, Nancy is having a problem with her dad. I suggested she talk with you, to help her straighten it out. Is that okay?"

"Of course," I said. "If she likes, I'll try.

Nancy and I talked, and Bernie joined the conversation. The four of us learned a great deal about each other that evening.

Just before high school graduation, Mark and Nancy announced they were very much in love and wanted to marry in the near future. I begged them to give that decision a lot of thought and I threw every reason in the book at them to show that step was premature. "Unless Nancy's pregnant," I said.

"No, Mom! She isn't!" Mark exclaimed. I exclaimed, "Thank God!"

Their engagement would be announced just before they left for college. Nancy was going to the University of Pennsylvania and Mark to Ithaca College in New York state.

Again, I begged them. "You have been seeing each other steadily for almost two years now. Give yourselves a chance to be apart. When you come home for Thanksgiving, then, at that point, make your decision."

There was much talk, time, and thought thrown around on this very serious subject for weeks. They finally agreed to my logic. I don't know how Nancy's parents felt about it, however, as we never discussed it with them. Bernie and I took a "sit back and wait" attitude at that point.

They were going to wait until Thanksgiving vacation to make their decision. When they came home in November, for the holiday, Nancy informed Mark she had become engaged to a boy she met at college. The reason she did not call or write to him about it was that she wanted to tell him in person.

Mark was devastated. He did not talk to us very much about it, after the initial shock. He returned to college and proceeded toward his career.

Through his letters and our telephone conversations, we learned he was dating. There were many girls he mentioned, but none in a serious vein. He remained friends with them over the years, and later in time, would often meet with one of the girls and her husband for an evening out, to talk about "the good old days."

He never mentioned Nancy again to us.

After completing two years at Ithaca College, on a scholarship as a drama major, Mark was very active in all phases of the theater, including summer stock in Clinton, New Jersey, for two seasons. He discovered his forte was not in front of the camera or on the stage. His ability to communicate was best served behind the scenes, perhaps directing, producing, or public relations.

In the fall of 1971, he entered Emerson College, in Boston, where he majored in speech and mass communications. Among many activities, he became Director of Public Affairs and Public Relations, a campus radio show host, a theater and film critic, and a member of the Musical Theater Society.

In setting up his classes for the fall of 1972, he called home full of enthusiasm and excitement. "Mom! Dad! I think I can graduate in three and a half years instead of four years of college!"

Bernie joined the conversation on an extension phone as I interrupted to ask, "Mark, how could you do this, especially since you changed colleges? From what I know, a student usually loses credits somewhere along the line."

"True, but I had a meeting with my advisor, and with my credits from two years at Ithaca, plus the credits I've accumulated here at Emerson, and those I'll earn this semester, I'll qualify for graduation in January 1973.

"This will give me six months advantage for job hunting before the influx of June graduates. I'll have to go back in June 1973 for the graduation ceremonies."

"Mark, this is your mother talking," I said. "This sounds great, terrific and we're so proud of you, but, just double check to be sure you're not disappointed."

We all laughed and he said, "Okay! Okay, Mom! Shall do!"

"Love you! Bye!" we told him.

Living at home in New Jersey, the six months before June graduation, Mark commuted into New York daily, and sometimes twice a day, job hunting and for interviews. He devoted a lot of time on research into former graduates of Ithaca and Emerson colleges to find out what they were doing in the communications field. It was not long before his perseverance paid off.

He made contact with a TV personality who had graduated from Ithaca College a few years earlier. The newscaster was so impressed with Mark's charisma and qualifications that he endorsed him and Mark was hired by a major national TV network. His career in public relations had begun.

In June 1973, Mark received his bachelor of arts and science, magna cum laude, plus other honors: deans list every semester, Gold Key award and a listing in the *National Publication of Who's Who Among Students in American Universities and Colleges 1972-1973.*

In time, Mark was asked to become producer for a well-known radio talk show host in New York City. Simultaneously, a position opened up for him at Prentice-Hall, publishers in Englewood Cliffs, New Jersey. Although he was then living in Manhattan, sharing an apartment with a college friend and traveling into New Jersey would be a chore, he decided it was worth the inconvenience because it offered a better opportunity in public relations.

Part of his work in the new position was to travel with authors and to publicize their books on TV, radio, and in the newspapers throughout the country.

Eventually, Mark made the decision to specialize in public relations for the theater. He would have to apprentice for about three years for an agency involved only in Broadway shows. He followed this through and worked himself up to vice president at an agency. Then, in December 1982, he opened *Mark Goldstaub Public Relations Agency.*

CHAPTER ELEVEN

Understanding Homosexuality

Most of us have been reared with the idea that there is only one proper, normal, acceptable form of sexual relationship— that between a man and a woman. And yet, there is in every individual, in some degree, an interest in a potential affection for members of the same sex, as well as for the opposite sex.

Because we have feared this in ourselves, because many of us wear a cloak of guilt and shame because of adolescent homosexual experimentation, we have set up psychological blocks against looking into and openly discussing the dual nature of human sexuality.

Only recently have we engaged in public discussion of this heretofore *hush-hush* topic. The growing climate of candor has been encouraged, for the most part, by homosexual organizations. Homosexuals have been "coming out of the closet" and politically lobbying for rights of homosexuals to hold jobs, marry, raise children and other normal life activities in a civilized society. They have also worked to have discriminatory laws against homosexuals taken off the books.

The uncertainty and controversy as to what causes homosexuality, or when it surfaces, whether it be genetic, constitutional, glandular, or from other, unknown factors, has been and remains debatable in the medical and mental health fields. There also seems to be much "incomprehensibility of God's actions," from the standpoint of many people.

Many youngsters recognize their homosexual tendency at age four or five. Others discover it in late adolescence or early adult life. Some homosexuals marry mates of the opposite sex in an attempt to "cure" themselves, but this rarely works.

In this experience called "life," the more people we can love, be friends with, be close to, accept for themselves—regardless of their sexual lifestyles,—the richer, healthier and happier our existence can be!

Society is not structured along the lines of monolithic moral values, but rather, on pluralism, which permits viable alternatives in ways of living and loving, as long as these alternatives do not infringe on the rights and freedoms of others. Closing the door on freedom in one group today will jeopardize the freedom of others tomorrow. Many homosexuals have made outstanding contributions to our culture, for example, in arts, music, science and humanities.

* * * * *

Our home in Clark, New Jersey, was a two-bedroom, two-bath, luxury garden apartment. It has a large screen-in terrace, swimming pool and tennis court. Once the boys, Mark and Paul, had left the nest, we no longer needed such a large house. We reluctantly sold it, and I emphasis *reluctantly* because we loved it. The approximately 10 years we lived there were healthy, happy, prosperous, wonderful years. We thought with our heads instead of our hearts, that the logical, practical thing to do was to sell it. And when we left there, it was with tears in our eyes.

On Father's Day (June 1977), Mark came to spend a special day with his dad. The weather was warm but comfortable. Paul also telephoned from out of state to wish his father greetings of the day. Everyone was happy and successful in their chosen careers. Happy, healthy, devoted children, we had. What more can parents ask for?

After lunch, we went for a swim, sat in the sun for a while, relaxed and enjoyed the serenity of the day in a loving atmosphere. We had dinner at home, rather than buck the holiday crowds at a restaurant. The three of us sat at the kitchen table and talked about Mark's work, his plans for the future and about friends. He always asked about the lives of his and our friends from his growing up years.

Being the era of the Anita Bryant tirade, it was natural for the conversation to turn in that direction. We expressed our opinions back and forth on homosexuality and were in complete accord. Anita Bryant, in those years, was totally wrong in her hostile attitude regarding sexual preferences. She had no right to dictate how anyone should live their own life.

During our discussion, I shared what I knew about a friend of ours from way back, Marty. He was a fine, warm individual and he had given loving care and attention to his widowed mother over the years (at the time, she was in her eighties). He and his lover had lived in California for the past 20 years.

We had admired and respected Marty for the way he handled his homosexuality, as well as his kind consideration of his aging mother. Mark remembered hearing Marty's name mentioned, over the years, but he had never met him and did not know Marty was gay.

"Mark," I explained, "back in those days, homosexuals were considered *perverts.*"

Mark said, "Let's get out of the kitchen and go relax on the terrace. It is such a beautiful night. Besides, I have something of *great importance* to tell you! Something I've wanted to share with you for a long time.

I immediately asked, "Mark, are you okay? Is there something wrong?"

"No! No!," he said. "Relax!"

As we comfortably seated ourselves outside, there was a delightful breeze. Mark sat down, facing Bernie and I. He reached out, took our hands and made his declaration:

"Mom and Dad, I'm just going to come right out with it. *I'm an active homosexual.* I have been since I was 17- or 18--years-old. That was when I had my first experience with a man.

"I'm not going into any details about it, but after being with you both today, listening to your feelings about homosexuals, and even though we've talked about homosexuals and gays before, I've been waiting for the opportune time—the best time—for you to handle it. I feel the time is now. You have given me my lead.

"I've wanted to tell you for years, and I've hated myself for keeping this from you for all these years," he continued as Bernie and I listened carefully and with caring. "But, I also don't want to live a lie any longer. Most importantly, I never have wanted to hurt either of you.

"I love you both, and God knows, I wish I could spare you the agony I know you must both feel at this moment. But, I now know, from what you've said about your old friend, Marty, and from your opinion of Anita Bryant's anti-homosexual campaign, that you will accept, understand, and support me. I certainly do need that!"

We all felt close as a family, and we each were computing in our minds what to say next. Mark continued with his revelation to Bernie and I:

"I apologize for breaking this to you, Dad, on your *special day,* but, I just felt in my gut that I have to get this heavy burden off my back today, and live more happily with myself. I have been seeing a psychiatrist for years, since just after I graduated from college.

"I wasn't able to admit my *homosexuality*—even to myself. I hated myself. I had to learn to accept, love and respect myself. And I had to regain my self esteem. Now that you both know, I can go on and live a successful life. With your *blessings*, I can have the right to be *me.*

We soon learned that telling parents what Mark told us is the most emotional and significant event in the life of a homosexual man. It is, perhaps, the ultimate test of love and understanding—for both the man and his parents.

Mark paused, from time to time during his conversation with Bernie and I, trying hard to keep his emotions under control. Several times, as we listened, I reached out to touch him and console him, but before either of us could say a word, he would go on.

"Mom, Dad, not your son's homosexuality, but the kind of human being you raised and nurtured is *important*. I'm still the same son you had before. I still love the beauty of the sunrise and the sun as it sets beyond the horizon.

"My sexual life (he did not say *preference*) has nothing to do with *who I am*. I've made love with women and men. My *biological need*, however, is most satisfied by a male and that makes me happy."

Bernie and I were experiencing a plethora of emotions as Mark told us everything, for the first time. At that time in America, however, labels "*homosexual*" and "*gay*" were becoming household words. But, as liberal as Bernie and I were, Mark's four words, "*I am a homosexual*", turned our lives into a turmoil.

HOMOSEXUAL—just a word in a dictionary—is something our society batters. *Gay,* another word, means "*happy, carefree, free of worry*". But, when the words came from Mark, in close communication with us, they hit home! His information made him feel relieved, but for us, it threw our inner beings out of control.

It was as though lightening had struck us between the eyes. There has not yet been a word coined to describe what his disclosures did to us, initially. Although I must admit we suspected his homosexuality, we had vehemently denied to ourselves that it could be true. We simply and repeatedly brushed the though of it out of our minds.

Mark's appearance, actions, and body motions never indicated homosexual characteristics, as we imagine these to be. From our limited knowledge at the time, we understood that homosexuals always show "effeminate tendencies."

No! That was not Mark! He was strong, male, and American! Looking back, we see how we screened out what we did not want to see.

After we sort of composed ourselves, I ventured to say, "Mark, you can't mean this. Surely, this is just something that will pass. It must just be something you want to experience temporarily. It must be related to some kind of curiosity about males and females. Well, that's okay, but . . ."

As the words poured out of my mouth, trying to understand his dilemma and, at the same time, trying to put my own mind back together, a former event in Mark's life suddenly flashed in my mind.

"This is all because of Nancy, isn't it?" I asked about his high school sweetheart.

"Well, Mark, my son, we all have gone through broken love affairs in our lives. This is the learning process of life. Please, son, realize that if you give it a chance, time heals all wounds.

"Open your mind to other women. There are plenty out there who would love to be *Mrs. Mark Goldstaub.* Open your mind to falling in love.

"You'll be just fine, I know. You'll be respected, loved, and a successful, humane being. The world is your oyster.

"Don't blow it because of a lost love that created a dislike and distrust for all women.

"Son," I told him with all the love a mother has, "we hear so often about people who use the expression *we made love,* but that is such a misconception. You just told us you have made love with men and women, but that your male partner made you happier.

"Mark, you didn't make love," I explained to him. "You simply had sex and satisfied a biological urge that you mistook for love or happiness.

"Mark, my son, you *make love* when you feel a deep, strong, passionate emotional affection for a person of the opposite sex. As you no doubt felt for Nancy, "making love" with someone you love makes you happy. It makes you happy enough to want to marry and share the rest of your lives with one another.

"You could have fathered her children! You could have followed the *natural* runway of life. Be honest with yourself, Mark!" I challenged him to consider.

"Does the sex you have with your male partners give you the same happiness you had making love with Nancy? No," I believed, "because it is just *sex and not love.*"

Mark took a turn to respond. "Mom! Mom! Calm down! Calm down! I know what you're saying, but I'll find that love with a man. Right now, living alone, there is no one—no one I want to be with on a permanent basis.

Eventually, it may not happen. Only time will tell. I'll know when it's love. I'll find my happiness in a monogamous relationship. You've met my women friends. They know I'm gay, but we socialize and have honest, deep, platonic friendships.

"The same goes for my male friends, whom you have met, some gay, some straight. They all like both of you and you've told me you like them."

Bernie was quiet. Up to that point, he had not said a word. He just sat there, taking it all in. Then, suddenly, he commanded, "Mark! Syl! Slow down! You two've been going at this long enough. I have something to say that must be said. I want you to listen very carefully, Mark.

"The generation I come from views homosexuals with disdain and contempt. People can be cruel and ugly. It is most essential for you to realize this, my son. Your career, your life, above all, your state of mind may be jeopardized. "You will hear comments from people who are unaware you are gay, who always have something to say about *fags, queers, fruit cakes* and so on. Sometimes, wise guys will crack jokes and a whole room full of people will be laughing. Will you be laughing with them?

"Down deep inside you, it will hurt like hell. What Mom said about Nancy and your reorganizing your lifestyle to be heterosexual makes a lot of sense. I know you can do it.

"The intelligent, determined, disciplined and compassionate manner with which you've managed your life to this point proves you have the capacity to do what is best for you and your future.

"And Mom did a darn good job of preparing you and Paul to handle yourselves when the time came to get out on your own. I say Mom, because I was away working practically seven days a week. I'm proud of all three of you, Sylvia, Paul and Mark. You are the most important people in my life."

Mark said, "Thanks Dad! It means a lot to me to hear you say that. Listen, Dad, homosexuality has been going on for 5,000 years, or more. Who knows? It is not something that happened 20 or 30 years ago. It is here, a fact of life. People have become more open and they're admitting to their sexual needs and coming out of the closet.

"I am very aware of all you've said, believe me. I have gone the whole gamut, with my psychiatrist. I am what I am. I hope you two will accept that as it is.

"I love you both, so please be happy for me and wish me health and happiness. Though I don't understand, from what you said about your friend, Marty, and Anita Bryant, I got the message you understand and accept!"

I interrupted. "Son! Just a second. Yes, we do understand and have empathy for homosexuals, but when it *hits home,* it touches parents' hearts. It takes on a whole different dimension. A parents chemistry—I don't know what the hell to call it— wants their child to be healthy, happy, successful, accepted, damn it, not set up for ridicule. We don't want to see you laughed at, an object of mockery, and God knows what!

"You have to watch what you do, what you say, the stress and strain every minute. Looking over your shoulder for fear you will be fired because the boss, a co-worker, or someone has found out you are not straight.

"When these things happen, and they will, what will this do to that wonderful free spirit, drive and determination you possess? It has to take its toll. Everything you persevered for may be lost. Society isn't ready to accept."

Mark explained, "Mom, in my business everyone is involved in one way or another with homosexuals. You'd be surprised. They don't even give it a thought. You are over emphasizing the whole picture. You see only one side.

"You're asking me to give heterosexuality a chance, and I have. You don't know how hard I've tried. As I said before, I've been seeing my psychiatrist for years. I'm still seeing her, and ironically, her name is *Sylvia.*"

Mark didn't give her last name and neither of us asked. We respected his privacy.

We were emotionally drained and it was getting late. Mark had to get back to the city. We hugged, kissed and wished him well as we said good night. Bernie gave Mark one last word as we walked him to the door.

"Please, dear son, be discreet. Keep it under wraps and do yourself and us a favor."

"Okay, Dad! Okay!" Mark said.

Bernie and I didn't get much sleep that night. We spent most of the night trying to convince each other that Mark would make every effort to overcome his homosexual attitude. Our lack of knowledge of homosexuals, at the time, was clouding our senses.

Mark and I spoke every few days, via telephone, but not much in the way of more understanding could be accomplished that way.

It was about three weeks later, when he suggested, "Mom, how about my coming out for the weekend? I'll get there in time for Friday night dinner and I'll stay through Sunday after dinner. Maybe we can take a ride out to an antique show or maybe a flea market just like we used to." Mark knew how Bernie and I loved antiques.

"Okay," I agreed wholeheartedly. "That sounds great. We'll see you Friday night!"

After dinner that Friday, Mark talked excitedly about the Broadway shows he was representing through the agency he was working for at the time. His apprenticeship was progressing nicely. Other than those conversations, we spent most of the evening watching television. Nothing was mentioned about homosexuality, except when I asked him, "Have you ever talked with Paul about yourself?"

Mark answered, "No. I wanted you and Dad to know first."

I asked, "Do you want us to tell him?"

"No," he explained. "I'll tell him. I'll let you know when I do. Paul and I have good rapport and we get along fine. I respect him and like him. I know he feels the same way about me. We have good talks together by phone, and I know it will be okay with him."

I was glad to hear that and I told Mark so.

"Mom," he said to change the subject. "Let's not talk about *me* for the weekend. I want to just *be with* you two guys and *relax*".

Saturday morning, Bernie went to his office and Mark and I had breakfast. As we were clearing the table, he said, "I know I said I did not want to talk about myself all weekend, but I just want you to know I have discussed everything that you and Dad said to me, during our last visit, with my psychiatrist. I'm very happy all that is behind me."

I gave Mark a hug and kiss for encouragement. "Mark! That is terrific. I knew you would do what was *right for you*. You are too smart and wise to ruin your life. And, that is a great weight off our hearts.

"You won't be sorry! You'll meet the right girl, get married and have the children you always wanted."

Mark interrupted to say, "Wait! Wait, Mom! You aren't *listening* . . . I said I was happy! Happy with my life."

In my need to have Mark lead a heterosexual lifestyle, I had immediately assumed that, if he had talked with his psychiatrist, he had embraced Bernie's and my logic.

"Are you telling me . . . ?" I asked with a weaker voice.

"Yes, Mom. I'm telling you I am a confirmed homosexual and nothing in this world can change it. I hope you and Dad will accept and live with it. Anyway, I know we'll always love each other and be happy. You'll see!"

I was angry, confused, and hurt. I told him, "I guess there is nothing more I can say."

He agreed. "Nothing, Mom. Let it be."

I felt myself tensing up. My mind was racing and my whole being seemed to be churning, churning. I was losing control. I wanted to scream, grab him and shake some sense into his head. I knew that if he and I didn't get out of the house, among some other people, there would be a terrible battle.

To avoid a confrontation, I took a deep breath, as calmly as possible, and suggested, "Let's go take our showers, get dressed, then go roam around the mall for a couple of hours. Is there anything you need from a store?"

"I don't know, Mom, but the mall sounds like a good idea."

"Your dad will be home early tonight to spend time with us," I said as I left him to go get ready.

We had an afternoon together that day that was not "the best of times." And at dinner, Mark told Bernie about our morning talk. Not much more was said because the tension was "so thick you could cut it with a knife."

We were under indescribable stress. We sat in silence as we watched television that night. We were going through the motions of trying to be sociable, but the upheavals in our systems had created a total blank.

After Sunday breakfast, Mark felt it best that he leave instead of spending the rest of the day with us, as he had earlier planned.

One week, two weeks, three weeks, four weeks went by. I had not heard from him, nor did I attempt to call him. I would venture to say we were going through a "cooling off" period by unspoken mutual consent.

Bernie and I were hurt, angry, disappointed, confused and heartsick. Our previously happy world had fallen apart. Bernie became more and more withdrawn. At night, after dinner, he would sit alone in the dark and cry.

Bernie blamed himself for not spending more time with his son when Mark was growing up. He felt he had failed as a father. He kept wondering if there was something he had done to cause his son to become homosexual.

I sat for hours on the floor, at the foot of his chair, consoling him. I tried to draw him into conversation and I attempted to re-establish his self esteem. I tried to reinforce his feelings of self worth. I held him in my arms every night while he cried himself to sleep.

How Bernie was able to continue getting up every morning, function, go to work, put in profitable days, I'll never know. At the same time, I realized that if it had not been for his work, I would have had a *basket case* on my hands.

"I feel so guilty, Syl," he would say. "Mark's homosexuality is my fault. While he was growing up, I never took him fishing, camping, hunting or participated in lots of other activities that fathers and sons do together. Maybe being exposed to all of those things, early in life, would have leaned him in a different direction."

I would tell Bernie, "Don't degrade yourself. You are a hard-working, warm, loving, devoted father and husband. Your sons love you, admire you, respect you and appreciate you. They also *like* you.

"And I love, admire, respect and appreciate you. And, oh yeah," I added lightly, "I *like* you too. You know that not everyone who is loved is also liked? You are special, Bernie! Don't you ever forget that!"

"You are allowing self blame to cloud your memory. There were many activities you shared with both our sons," I reminded him.

Our talks continued for days and nights as weeks went by. We relived many past happenings.

One evening, I said, "Bernie, even though you worked long hours [he was sales manager for a home improvement company], you managed to make yourself available to attend Boy Scouts meetings for both Mark and Paul. Mark was so proud when you volunteered to be Quartermaster of his troop.

"And, remember, I asked what *quartermaster* was and you answered, 'I don't know either, but I'm sure to find out at the next meeting when I assume the post'."

We laughed as we recalled that incident, and I was grateful to hear Bernie chuckle again. It had been a while since he had.

At another time, I reminded him, "You and Mark loved the Mets baseball team and sat through many a game together in front of the TV. You would both yell, scream, and curse the players. And you both would laugh your heads off at the stupid game.

"Speaking of the Mets," I added, "how about the times you took Mark and his clique to Shea Stadium with that large banner they had made from a bedsheet? Remember? The boys had painted it with big letters: *METS! LET'S GO METS!*" It took about eight kids to support the darn thing! No, Bernie you were not at fault."

I made every effort to bring up the many good quality hours Bernie and Mark had spent together during Mark's growing up years. I tried to draw Bernie out of his depression.

After many attempts at getting him to go for counseling, he confessed to me, "Syl, many times during the day, I park on the side of the road, sit, cry and talk to myself. I ask myself questions, for which I sometimes have answers and sometimes don't.

"I am my own psychiatrist. It helps me get through the day. I have been doing this for weeks. It has been my salvation."

I questioned him about that. "Dear, during these talks, do you ask yourself about the quality times you spent with Mark? Do you give yourself positive thoughts?"

He answered, "It's funny you should ask me that. Just today, I thought of the time I taught him how to ride his first two-wheeler. When I removed the training wheels, and ran next to him ready to grab him if he fell, I suddenly recalled that I never learned to ride a bicycle. Yet, I taught Mark! I was proud of us both!"

I reminded Bernie of other times. "How about the Sundays we four played tennis at Dehart Park? Mom and son against Dad and son! That was in the days that tennis wasn't so popular. Boy! Didn't we have fun? Bernie," I said sincerely, "you were darn good at tennis!"

I had become more and more concerned about Bernie's health, but could not convince him to visit our doctor. He was not eating properly, and he was losing weight. He looked *awful.*

During those tormenting weeks, we cut down on our socializing. Our friends, of course, wondered about us. They noticed we were not the same happy, joking Sylvia and Bernie. Humor has long been our best friend!

A tone of voice often reveals many emotions—one's ups and downs, sads and glads. Living through our horrendous traumà,we did a tremendous job pretending all was well every time we spoke with Paul. We kept our voices high-spirited, as in the past, but we hated the deception. Paul wanted to be kept well informed about *everything* that was happening in our family.

"Mom, even though I am hundreds of miles away, I want to know," he explained. "I'm part of the family, and it's only fair to tell me the good, bad, whatever."

But, I couldn't tell him about Mark. Paul, our first-born son, and I couldn't discuss that until Mark had revealed his lifestyle to Paul. Bernie and I handled it very well every time Paul talked to us about his many conversations with Mark. Paul was very proud of his "little brother," we knew, and we thought when Mark told Paul, everything would be fine.

My intuition told me when Paul learned of the events of the preceding few months. We knew that he, also being a warm, compassionate, loving young man, would understand Bernie's and my actions.

One evening during dinner I noticed Bernie's face turn red.

"Dear, are you feeling all right?" I asked. "Your face is red!"

He brushed me off at first. "It's nothing! My face feels very hot once in a while, for the last couple of days, but it goes away."

I said, "This is it. Whether you like it or not, you are going to the doctor. I'm calling first thing in the morning."

His general condition was satisfactory, but he developed high blood pressure and, understandably, he was given medication which we hoped would control the pressure.

While with the doctor, I told him everything that had taken place. He had been our family doctor for years and knew Mark. I was always comfortable with him and it was cathartic for me to talk to someone. He did his best to ease the pain for both of us. He made a special effort to give Bernie a bit of a lecture about guilt.

On the way home, I said, "Bernie, I have an idea, from listening to the doctor talk to you about guilt. Why don't we go to the library and see what books we find on homosexuality? Maybe Mark is right. We don't know much about it. Perhaps I am grabbing at straws, but I have to do something constructive to get our lives back into some semblance of order."

"Sylvia," Bernie said, "it's getting late and I'm worn out from the exam and the anxiety. I'd rather go home."

The next morning, I was at the library as soon as it opened. I spent day after day doing research on homosexuality. I sat in the reference room for hours at a time, reading books, magazines and medical journals. I also listened to audio tapes. Because the reference materials could not be checked out, I took notes. And, my mind was a sponge.

At night, I would sit with Bernie and go over my notes and other library books which I had checked out. We studied every aspect, analytically. We "crammed a lifetime of education" into the three months since our last contact with Mark.

The most important, vital thing we learned was that Mark, our flesh and blood son, was going through the worst torture of all. He had far more to contend with than his mother and father. He was living a nightmare.

It was his life, regardless of how we reacted. Mark needed us, our support and love to help him through the rough spots— and there were many. Mark had been right when he told me, "You don't know enough about homosexuality."

We are forever grateful we made the effort and learned. Education and information are the keys to understanding.

The young man who made the following statement committed suicide at age 20. His words are for all mankind!

If you could listen to the inner thoughts of a homosexual child, you might hear something like this:

"I can't ever let anyone find out that I'm not straight. It would be so humiliating. My friends would hate me. I just know it. They might even want to beat me up. And my family? I've overhead them lots of times talking about gay people. They said they hate gays, and that God even hates gays too. Gays are bad, and God sends bad people to hell. It really scares me when I hear my family talk that way because, they are talking about me. I guess I'm no good to anyone . . . not even God. Life is so cruel, and unfair. Sometimes I feel like disappearing from the face of this earth . . ."

No one chooses their sexual identity. If you are teaching your child to hate homosexual people, you might be teaching one of them to hate themselves.

* * * * *

One afternoon about 2 o'clock, Bernie called. "Hi Dear!" I'm glad I caught you at home. I'll be there in half an hour. I have something very important to tell you!"

"Are you okay?" I anxiously asked.

"Yes! Yes! I'm okay. Bye!" He hung up.

It was most unusual for him to come home in the afternoon, and many crazy thoughts raced through my mind. I impatiently waited at the window to see him drive in; and the moment he got out of the car, I saw the change in his face—it was not so drawn.

He looked relaxed, and his body moved faster. As he came closer, and into the house, I could sense an almost total change in him.

He kissed me and held me close.

135

"What is it?" I wanted to know. "What happened?"

"Syl, this afternoon I did the usual. I pulled the car over to the side of the road and had my private talking session, but I didn't cry today. I asked myself questions, but it was different today. It was like a cleansing, and suddenly, I knew.

"I am not at fault. I am not to blame. I've been a good father. I am a good father!

"You know what suddenly came to my mind? The many Sunday mornings, when the boys were small, and I would let you sleep while I took them out to breakfast at the Weequahic Diner—just us three guys.

"They loved it when I allowed them to do their own ordering. It made them feel *grown up*. Then, sitting in the car this afternoon, I relived the Sunday morning Mark went with me on a call to a prospective customer. He was about eight years old.

"He dressed up in a shirt, tie, and sport jacket, and he carried my briefcase. He was ready for business!

"Remember when we came home that day, and I told you what he had done? I can still see him sitting at the kitchen table, in the customer's house. First, he caught my eye, then he glanced at something on the table. It was one of my competitor's business cards. Boy, was I proud of him for that, and I let him know it later."

I remembered how Mark loved calling on customers with Bernie. "You know," I said, "Mark's going with you, and observing how to communicate with customers, could have established a foundation for him in dealing with the public in his career.

"Bernie I think you're just great, and so does Mark! You didn't fail your son. He learned from a master!"

"Syl, that is exactly what I realized today. I did not fail my sons." He laughed and added, "Just call me Dr. Goldstaub, the private psychiatrist."

Bernie continued. "This is the way I solve my problems, talking to myself. Everybody has their own way. I'm going to be fine."

Before I could say any more, Bernie went on. "There is another thing I resolved. I had been thinking maybe there was something within me, physically, that caused Mark to become gay. But, *no way*.

"From what we learned from all your research, reading and analysis, that is ludicrous. Does one really know, even science, what cause man to love man and woman to love woman, anymore than for woman to love man and man to love woman? We fall in love with a person—not a penis or vagina."

I was so proud of Bernie that I was bursting with joy! Having this knowledge well established in our minds, our hearts aching to see Mark, we agreed he should know how much our feelings had changed.

"I'm going to call and invite him for the weekend," I said.

Bernie questioned, "Do you think he'll accept?"

I called that evening to find out.

"Mom!" Mark exclaimed. "It's so good to hear your voice. Yes! I sure would love to see you and Dad. It has been too long! How are you both doing? Feeling okay I hope?"

I told him, "Yes, now, we're both fine. We will fill you in when you get here."

Bernie picked up the extension and said, "Hello son! How are you doing?"

"Fine, Dad. It's sure good to hear your voice too. I'll see you guys Saturday, around one o'clock. I have a business appointment in the morning, at the office, then I'll grab the bus into Jersey from there. I'll plan to spend the night."

"Swell. See you soon," Bernie said. I added, "We love you."

"Mom, I needed to hear that! Today is Wednesday. I'll see you in three days. And, I really love you both!"

Waiting for those three days to pass was like waiting a lifetime! When Mark arrived, we were so pleased to see him looking so well. As soon as we greeted, I began telling him about the research I had done, and how Bernie got interested. I told Mark everything else we had gone though—the good, the bad, the anger, disappointment, and most importantly, our *acceptance*.

"You were right, Mark. We did not know enough about the homosexual person. We were pupils, but now we have become teachers."

Mark was deeply touched and started to cry, but quickly regained his composure. He assured his dad, "There was never anytime in my life that I felt you failed me. Paul and I were very

137

much aware of how hard you worked, and we admired and respected you for it.

"And, we were always proud of you too, Mom. I want the both of you, at this moment, to know I'm especially proud of you for what you've accomplished these past few months. It sure wasn't easy, I know."

Mom, dad and son had not been so happy and felt so great for months. We kissed and hugged all weekend.

After we had talked, Mark said he was going to tell Paul and his wife. "As a matter of fact, I have to be in Minneapolis next week. Maybe they can meet me at the hotel and we'll have a nice weekend together?"

I thought that would be great, but I requested, "Mark, please don't tell him about what Dad and I have been through. I think it's only fair to Paul that we tell him."

Mark and Bernie both agreed with that.

We had dinner early that Sunday, and as we were leaving our apartment to walk Mark the two and one half blocks to the bus stop, I thought to myself, sometimes a father and son need private moments together. Realizing Bernie and Mark had found a new closeness and understanding, I suggested, "Why don't you two go without me. I'll get started cleaning up the kitchen."

I think they both read my mind, for without much protest, they agreed.

I kissed Mark goodbye and wished him well. He said he would call to let us know he arrived home safely.

I stood at the open door and watched as they walked down the path. Bernie had his arm around Mark and I heard him say, "Welcome home, Son!"

Mark kissed his dad, turned back toward me and called out, "Mom, we have quite a guy here! You two make a great pair. I always knew I came from good stock! Bye again! I love you both!" He most often said those words when leaving or ending a telephone conversation.

The following Saturday night, we received a call from Paul and his wife. They were at the hotel with Mark. He had told them about his homosexuality, and that we knew and accepted.

138

They wanted us to know all was well, and that they were very proud of us and sent their love.

After the call, Bernie and I looked at each other, then held each other closely. For the first time in months, we were able to breathe easily and relax.

I called Paul the following Monday night and Bernie joined us on the extension. Paul explained, "I surmised Mark was gay, but wasn't prepared to discuss it with you and Dad. My brother is my brother. I love and accept him, regardless of his lifestyle. I'm very glad he decided to make his disclosure. Now that we all know, we'll all be happier. As we told you the other night, we are so proud of you two."

"Thank you Paul," I said. "Mark had requested we not say anything to you about his being gay, because he wanted to tell you. I asked him not to say anything to you about our reactions to his disclosure. We all felt that was fair to each other."

I related to Paul the events of the preceding three months, for Bernie and I. Paul was forgiving, sympathetic and a tower of strength.

Paul said, "I'm just sorry I wasn't able to be there to help you and Dad navigate the troubled waters." He said we had his full support and that he'd always be there for us.

"Call me to talk, anytime, even at the office at the college. You have the number. From now on, everything is out in the open. I understand you had no choice, and that you were obeying Mark's request.

"I respect you for that and forgive you, so don't be concerned about it. We all love each other. Let's put the pieces of our lives back together and be a complete family again. It's time to go on with living!"

We did just that! For the next nine or ten years, we had smooth sailing. What was past was past.

As the philosopher, Baruch Spinoza once said, "*It's not the laughter or the tears that is important—it's the understanding!*"

CHAPTER TWELVE

A Father's Tribute To His Son

By Bernie Goldstaub

The fact that my son was homosexual initially disturbed me, but after coming to grips with reality, and realizing the enormous love a father has for his own son, I accepted him.

Mark was one of my two sons. Like his brother, Paul, Mark, is my flesh and blood, and was conceived with love and tenderness between his mother, Sylvia, and me.

Mark is who he is—a fine, compassionate, loving, caring humane being. I am, and always will be, proud of him, and proud to call him *my son.*

The magic carpet of happiness on which our family rode was yanked out from under us when Mark told us, Sylvia and I, "I have AIDS." I could not deny that AIDS is a terminal illness.

I continually asked myself, *"Why Mark? He is a super-special, young, loving man. Why Mark?"* People like him are so needed in this world. His genuine *goodness* is needed as well.

A day did not pass that I didn't look at the sky and beg and plead with God, "*Please! Please, let my son live. Take Me! Take me, but let him live. I have lived my life, let him live his, Lord.*"

Day and night I pleaded for this to happen. I became so angry with the world of science and so furious that more progress was not being made to find a cure for the AIDS plague.

I wondered, Why the *indifference* and *delay* and why people with AIDS are forced to buy their medication from sometimes underground networks to foreign countries. Is this because of *organized greed* by the powers that be?

Our young people have added so much to our culture, advancement and education, but too many of them are dying, while they spend tens of thousands of dollars for *hopes, dreams and medications which will postpone death.*

Throughout this ordeal, my heart constantly pounded and I could feel my blood rushing to my head. I managed to smile and instill some positive thoughts, however. Mark beat that, though, because he held off and he fought for so long. He always hoped a serum would be found to delay advancement of his AIDS. His attitude was so remarkable and beyond belief, that he still shields us.

Whenever we visited Mark, I tried to concentrate on *HUMOR.* Humor is "our best friend." I would tell him some corny jokes, which he always loved. And I was rewarded by his chuckles, and often, deep, hearty laughs!

Mark and I shared a hobby. We both loved to cook, but he is a *true gourmet.* At one point in time, I found my hobby to be a great way to burn off energy and keep my mind occupied. The kitchen was my escape from the "emotional war-zone."

A private joke evolved among friends and family about our kitchen skills: When in doubt about the proper seasoning for a recipe, whatever you're cooking, *just add garlic.* (Or even *more garlic.*) This became one of our kitchen jokes, just between Mark and I. Add garlic!

There were times when I felt like punching a hole in the wall, and there were other times I wanted to scream out the window, "God! You are so unfair! Why do you take the good, productive, young people?" You allow some people to live longer, but under what physical conditions? It is so unfair, Lord!"

But I managed to control my anger and my temper. The situation was so frightening, so gut-wrenching, that it broke my heart for a while.

We were all a family, however, so we kept the ball rolling. There were no quitters on the *Goldstaub Team!* Paul, Sylvia and I kept the mail flowing. I will always remember one letter I sent to Mark, in which I wrote, "We have loved you since the day you were born, and with each passing day, the love continues to grow."

Mark told me after reading it, "Dad, that letter was so full of love it may me cry."

After Mark died, my life as a father and husband continued, but I wore a mask. I knew Sylvia, Paul and I would never be the same, that we would never enjoy things as we did with Mark in our lives.

But, we kept on going, for each other and for him. His spirit and soul is still with us, and he will forever be in our hearts. I handled my bereavement the best way I could. My crutch was to remember the many, oh so many, good times.

But as Sylvia does, I, too, asked the question, "Why couldn't the good times have continued?"

I often have told myself, "Bernie, you *must* accept the things you cannot change. Show courage to change the things you can, and the wisdom to know the difference."

For a long time, I keep hearing Mark repeating, *"Be happy! Don't Worry! Keep on dancing, no matter how hard it gets!" Sylvia and I harnessed our pain and used it in constructive ways.*

I continued to work with the various AIDS support groups. It has been so very important to give them the moral support they so deeply need. I know Mark is aware of what his family continues to do, including Sylvia's lectures on the total need for family bonding.

No One Should Walk Away From Their Loved One, Because They Have Contracted AIDS!

They certainly didn't ask for it. Someone with AIDS needs others who care more than any other time in their lives. Parents need their children and each child needs its parent.

Sylvia's sister lives in Los Angeles. She insisted we visit with her for the summer. She said, "The change of scenery from Florida, and the interesting places to visit here, will be good for your morale." We accepted the invitation and arrived in Los Angeles in June 1990.

It was a bonus to learn son Paul also was invited to visit for part of the summer! He managed to rearrange some of his prior commitments to join us there.

Mark's former secretary, Virginia, was then living in Los Angeles, and she invited us to attend a Wednesday night Louise Hay Support Group Meeting.

"Bernie," she explained, "I attend as often as I can. I think you and Sylvia will find it most satisfying. People from all walks of life come, for all sorts of reasons."

At first, I hesitated to attend. I don't really know why. From our visits with Mark, I had learned about Louise Hay. We often sat with Mark and listened to her *Meditation and Healing Imagery* audio tape.

Sylvia, however, felt the need to go to the meeting, so off she went. And she dragged me with her.

Attending that meeting was the "best medicine" in the world for us at the time.

We were astonished to find at least 250, or more, there. There was so much pouring out of *love, caring and giving,* that everyone greeted each other with hugs and true, humane warmth.

During the course of the meeting, anyone who wished could stand up and say whatever they wanted to say about themselves. Some asked for help, others offered help. People ventilated every innermost thought and feeling one could have. Some cried. Some laughed. We, the audience, cry and we laugh.

Before we figured out what the customs were in the meetings, Sylvia quietly asked Virginia, "Is anyone allowed to speak?" Virginia explained to her, "Yes. Just raise your hand and someone with a microphone will come to you." [At the time, Sylvia was writing this book.]

Sylvia raised her hand and, eventually, a microphone was placed in front of her. She stood up, a bit nervously at first, but then she gradually calmed down and spoke to the audience

144

about the book, and about our love for Mark. She shared with the others there the stories we had been told by People With Aids (PWAs) and about our AIDS support groups back home.

Sylvia also told about families who had abandoned their children because of our *homophobic* society. She contrasted the *loving* parent with the *negative* parent. At the finish of her speech, she received a loud and long applause.

To our astonishment, after the meeting, we were surrounded by dozens of young people who hugged us, thanked us, and wanted to tell us about the negative attitude of their parents. Many of those youngsters had not heard from or seen their parents in years. Many wanted to tell their stories in Sylvia's book.

Perhaps, they may have thought, their parents would some day read it and then not be afraid to show love, acceptance and understanding.

Sylvia did incorporate some of these true, sometimes heartbreaking, stories, in her book. Both she and I hope there will be some parents who will read these stories and respond in a positive nature for the sake of all humankind. We especially hope for the young people we met at the Louise Hay meeting every Wednesday during our stay in Los Angeles.

Once, as we were meeting face to face with Louise, she told us, "So few parents come."

Sylvia and I were lifted to the heights of euphoria by the flow of love, support, and mutual understanding that always characterizes her meetings. I only wish I could package the emotions there and deliver it to every father in America!

I could feel the bright, shiny light and the sunshine of love blanketing everyone there. I was grateful I had the benefit of that experience. Even today, I miss each and every one of the "Louise Hay family."

Reach out to your loved ones. Help them with love. That was her message, and it is ours.

At our group meetings, young people with AIDS would come over to me and ask how they could get their father to accept them. All of them needed to be loved—not ignored or deserted.

They would desperately ask, "What can I do to be reunited with my father, and with my family?" They also showed understanding of their parents' plight. For example, many would ask, "Why can't my parents understand me?"

I talked to them and discussed a parent's point of view, as well as what I knew about the points of view of sons and daughters. I told them what I felt would work, in most cases.

I offered to help by speaking with their parents, thinking I could perhaps ease their situation from my personal experience. I did what I believed would help others—and I found that also helped me. It was all very worthwhile.

Then there came a day in my life when I suddenly realized I was on the road to becoming an *alcoholic*. When I was drinking, the feeling of numbness would be my escape from anguish and sorrow. The *high* which liquor gave me soothed my *heartache* temporarily. With growing knowledge that my drinking was turning me into an alcoholic, and the realization that this only added to the tragedy of our lives, I abstained.

Everything, I have learned, takes time, and time can't make a loss disappear. But I've been learning to accept things I can't change.

I never have played the "macho image" of the all-powerful father. In our family, we are *one for all and all for one!* Our family was a real, loving team.

It helped me to talk to myself. "Let it out," I told myself. "Get a handle on the situation! *Be There For Loved Ones!*"

I suppose I always will have some periods of feeling anger, sorrow and grief. But love helps me cope. I took time to *think* and to *find answers to my own questions.*

"Why? What?" I now know that *not all questions have answers.*

It is beyond my understanding why so few fathers attended our AIDS support group meetings. In the course of discussions, mothers outnumber fathers 10 to one. They tearfully open their hearts and ask, *Why can't our husbands accept and support their sons and daughters, who have AIDS, instead of walking away— and in some cases—resenting their wives for loving and accepting their mutual offspring.*

In fact, there were many men who resented their wives coming to our meetings. Those husbands wanted "nothing to do with the nightmare!"

In my wildest dreams, I will never comprehend how a real man, a father, could deny his love to his own *dying child.*

* * * * *

I could not finish *my tribute* to my son Mark without also giving tribute to his loyal companion for seven years, Edmund Wojcik.

Edmund gave love, compassion, and tenderness to Mark, and he knows Sylvia and I love him for that. He also knows we respect him and that we always will. He is a welcome member of our family.

I don't know if Sylvia, Paul and I could have survived the dark days which followed Mark's death if Edmund had not cared for us so much. It was he who selected the coffin, the chapel, and made every arrangement for the funeral services. Edmund took care of all the morbid details involved with funerals.

There are just no words to describe the additional excruciating pain we would have had to suffer if we had to do what he lovingly did for us.

There is a common supposition that *Parents Are Not Supposed To Outlive Their Children.*

The memorial chapel, where we last visited with Mark in person, was overfilled with sympathizers. They were standing three-deep at the rear of the chapel, up and down the stairway, and actually overflowing into the outside street and sidewalks area. We, the family, could feel the *sadness* of those who came— from far and wide—to pay their respects to Mark, our beloved son. It was so severe a loss to everyone!

* * * * *

Edmund said, during his eulogy to Mark, "We must remember what Mark accomplished on this earth. It was *so much* during his short time of thirty-seven years he was with us. He became successful, respected, and admired! He was so very loved and he left such a lasting impression on all who knew him.

"Most people don't accomplish this if they live twice his lifetime. I'm very proud to be a part of Mark's life. He loved everyone he touched. Everyone he touched also loved him."

147

I, Mark's father, have always been a *private person.* How do I explain this? Sometimes I don't have that answer, but I have been successful at *working things out my own way.*

I did that when I first learned, from Mark, that he was *gay.* I initially went off to be alone and work out those mixed feelings. Then, years later, when he told us he had AIDS, I was devastated.

I would sit by myself, in the darkness, on the terrace of our apartment—which overlooked a calm, private, secluded lake—and I would thoroughly *have it out* with the world's lack of justice.

I thought strongly and repeatedly, It's just not fair. I spent hours talking, thinking and asking such questions as, *Why do the good people suffer and the scum go on and on?"*

Other things I wondered were *What is justice? Where is justice?* And, I knew I could not change the world, so that meant that I must *accept the situation,*—for our family, for Mark and for others.

Mere words from me, in this or any other book, cannot ever describe the total heartbreak Sylvia and I experienced after Mark passed away. After that black time in our lives, I often awoke in the middle of the night and faced a midnight crisis, of sorts.

Once this happened, I opened my tired, sleepy eyes and looked around our bedroom, only to see Sylvia sitting in the corner of our bedroom, on the floor, crying and quietly asking herself, "Why? Why did this happen to our baby? Ohhhh! I can't live without him. I can't! And, I can't stand *the thought.*"

Those memories will never leave me. They will be constantly with me. I remember that, as I climbed out of bed, dead tired from work and stress, held her in my arms and coaxed her back to the security of our bed, I would repeat, *"We are here for each other—you, Paul and me."* We are here for each other: to love, help and understand. We need each other—you, Paul and myself. Our need for each other gives us the *strength and courage* to face tomorrow."

In the real world, most of us sustain ourselves by remembering all the times we shared with our sons, daughters, friends, companions, parents, siblings, etc. We talk, laugh, cry, remem-

148

ber, forget. We have sad times and glad times. We share anger and laughter. We have fun sometimes. Other times, tears flow. But, even in angry moments, *memories flow.*

Sylvia and I have often sustained ourselves by remembering all the times we shared with Mark and his companion, Edmund, and our other beloved son, Paul, and his wife. All the *fun things* and the *sad things*, yes, even the *angry* moments, now seem to be beautiful, flowing memories.

In my tribute to you, Mark Neil Goldstaub, I am *proud* to be your father. We—your mother, brother, lover and multitude of friends—who know your pure and true spirit and essence are, and will always be, with us all.

We miss you greatly. We love you more than words by voice or printing press can ever possibly express. And, we—one-by-one—will rejoin your presence at some future time. We will be together again.

With All Our Love,
Your Dad

CHAPTER THIRTEEN

I'm Gay! No You're Not!

Fred, a professor at a state university in Florida, and a friend of our family, related to me the history of his family's *estrangement* and *nonacceptance* of his homosexual orientation:

* * * * *

I never dealt with *being gay* until I was about 30 years old. I had been heterosexually married since I was 23. The marriage broke up when I was 30.

At that time in my life, I began to explore my full sexuality. Even though I had been brought up by a strict Catholic family, I knew I was homosexual. However, it was a very difficult thing to explore, as I was living in the midwestern United States at the time.

I found my definite attraction to other men very difficult to look into closely. I had known about my orientation since I was about six years old, and I had always considered it to be very natural—just normal—that all men felt the way I did.

I thought the difference between me and *gay people* was that they felt it even more strongly than I, and *acted on it.*

In my college years, I had gay friends who wanted a relationship with me, but I told them, "Thanks, but no thanks. I'm married."

I was sort of "hiding out" in the heterosexual marriage relationship.

However, the marriage didn't last, and after our divorce, I spent about a year figuring out what I wanted to do next with my life. I moved to Ann Arbor, Michigan, where I tried dating women, but that didn't work out. Then one day, I read this little classified advertisement in the University of Michigan's student newspaper:

> If you are gay or think you are gay
> or want to explore your sexuality,
> there is a group being formed.
> Call . . . the Student Counseling
> Center.

I called, and talked to a gay advocate for gay students. I learned that periodically he organized "coming out" groups of eight or 10 guys. The groups were headed by two counselors and they met weekly for about eight weeks.

The groups dealt with issues such as *gay identity*. The focus of the meetings was to present this in a very positive way, and help the group members form a positive gay identity. I initially felt the group experience would be very interesting, but I didn't act on it.

A couple of months later I saw the advertisement again. That was in 1982. That time, I thought, "Maybe I *should* check it out." I did. I remember going down to the counseling center and talking with people there.

They told me, "We can set you up for an appointment with one of our peer counselors." I agreed, and was scheduled to meet with two gay men who were leading one of the groups.

I was scared the first time I was in the group, talking about my being gay. But, as I came out, it really turned out to be a nice experience.

I remember one gay man telling about his lover, and I felt, "Don't use *that word* in front of me. I'm not ready for that yet."

152

After the meeting, I was excited. I thought, "Now it's okay for me to look at men!"

I went to a street-side cafeteria, where I just sat and looked at all the men going by. I even said, out loud, "Now it's okay!" It was really a very positive experience.

The group sessions concentrated on a lot of different issues. We left each meeting with a positive sense of ourselves as gay men. I always listened carefully to the stories from others as they struggled with coming out. I didn't have a great problem coming out. For me, it was a fantastic experience, and I was with a great group of people who were very supportive and very knowledgeable.

I lived in Ann Arbor for about three years and went through a couple of short-term relationships before I finally started a close relationship with Jim.

My parents were living just outside of Chicago, and I visited them every now and then and at Christmas. But I never told them I was gay.

My father died in 1984, and it took about a year for my mother to get over that. Also, at that time, I applied for my present job here in Florida. Things started to come together for me after that. I was hired and, since I was moving to Florida, Jim and I decided to break up, on friendly terms.

I came to Florida in January 1986, after going home for Christmas to visit with Mother, my brothers and sisters and other family members. While I was there, I had decided to tell Mother I was gay. Part of my motivation for telling her was that I knew she would want to come visit me in Florida, and I didn't want to have her come and see me in a situation where I had to have secrets about this or that. By that time, she had mostly recovered from my father's death. I was about 34 years old at the time.

We were driving home after church that Sunday, when I said, "Mom, I have to tell you something. I want you to know I am gay."

She had an incredibly bad reaction to my disclosure. She took it very poorly—to the extent that she disinherited me! She took away all the Christmas presents everyone had given me.

I had gone through that sort of reaction with others at the University of Michigan. There, I had even become a peer counselor and conducted my own coming out group. In a sense, I was sort of aware, through others in the group, about the difficulties of talking about this with their parents.

So, Mother's reaction did not overwhelm me. I decided to simply give her time.

Once I was in Florida, she and I often spoke on the telephone. And, when she came down to visit me, I thought she more or less accepted that I was gay. I guess, to put it another way, I realized she knew I was gay, but had decided not to pay any attention to that fact.

She never talked about it. Whenever I brought it up, she blocked it out. She didn't want to hear about it, from me or any of my gay friends.

About two years ago, during one of my Christmas visits back to Chicago, just as I was preparing to return to Florida, Mother said to me, "You know, Fred, my biggest wish is for you to find a girl and get married."

I reacted angrily and blurted out to her, "I'm sorry you can't accept who I am, but that is not my problem! If this is the situation, that's it!" I had tried so hard to have her understand and accept me the way I am.

The following Christmas, the same thing happened again. It devastated me. She didn't want to know anything about my life, about my being gay, about how I felt. She just wanted me to be the *nice young man* she always thought she had raised. While I was growing up, I was sort of a star—a super leader. She was really proud of this. I understood that, but I wondered why she couldn't *understand*.

At the time, I was teaching a course on the AIDS epidemic. I received newspaper coverage and television coverage. In those published and broadcast stories, I talked about my being gay, and how that was part of my teaching activities.

During Christmas 1989, I went to Chicago to visit Mother again. While I was there, I showed her videotapes from the broadcasts. She had already read newspaper stories about me. She was really excited about that. She wanted to show the stories to our relatives and her neighbors! When I found that out, I said,

154

"Mother, that's fine, for you to show the newspaper stories, but they say *I'm gay*."

She answered, "Oh no! They don't say that!"

I questioned her closely about her reading of what the news articles did say. "Mother, what do you mean. Did you read the articles carefully? Look! Right here, it says that I am gay."

She responded, "No! No! It doesn't say that!"

Mother was consistent about blocking it all out. I also realized the reason she was so interested in and excited about the television interviews and newspaper articles was the *publicity* about *her son.* To her, I was a *celebrity*.

For me, that was the final blow. I then realized she would never accept or even try to accept. So I began my own process of separation.

I decided I would no longer wait around for her to accept me. I tried to educate her by presenting her all the opportunities possible. I was *up front* with her and very supportive of her feelings. I also loved her, but I could no longer accept her attitude.

The night before I was supposed to leave Chicago, Mother started again on the "find a girl and get married" routine. We got into a nasty argument, and she yelled at me, "If you come down with AIDS, I hope your friends take care of you! I don't want to know anything about it!"

At that point, I told her I didn't want to maintain any more contact with her, and I stormed out of the house.

Since then, that is how our relationship has been. She has telephoned a couple of times, and I've talked to her and been civil. But, it was only *casual* talk.

I told my older brother, but I still don't know what he thinks. I told my sister. I thing she is the one I can talk to most, about this. I told my second oldest brother and got *no reaction*. I told my younger brother, and it turned out that he was the most accepting of all. He knows a lot of gay people.

This is rather funny, but I forgot to tell you that before I told Mother I was gay, I wanted to *prepare her.* I invited her and my sister to visit me in Ann Arbor, and meet my lover, Jim. I also wanted them to meet some of our friends.

Well, they stayed in our apartment, where we only had one bedroom. We let Mother and my sister sleep there, and Jim and I slept on the floor together, in the living room. No questions about that!

I took them to visit a good friend, Tom, who is about 10 years older than me. He is very handsome, a model, and he lives in a beautiful house in Ann Arbor. He fixed a fantastic lunch for us.

Tom has a beautiful garden and he spends a lot of time in it. He showed Mother and my sister all around his place. Mother, especially, was *pleased as punch.*

When she asked Tom, "Why don't you get married? You are so handsome and you have this gorgeous home?" Tom just laughed. He knew what was going on with Mother.

Well, anyway, what happened was that later, after we were back at our apartment, I told Mother, "All the people you met today, which you liked so much, are gay."

Again, she denied it. It was something she did not want to deal with. She responded, emphatically, "No, you're wrong! They're not gay!"

It remains one of "those situations." I have been in extensive therapy for the last few years, and it is working out very well for me. It has been through therapy that I have learned it is better for me to accept Mother the way she is than to go through all the feelings I have to go through to have her accept me.

She is a very important person in my life, and I do love her. She probably loves me, even though she prevents us having a good life together. So, for now, I just *let it be. So be it.*

The following letter is from the son of a fellow P-FLAG (Parents and Friends of Lesbians and Gays) member:

September 22, 1986

Dear Mom and Dad,

Although I thanked you on the phone, I wanted to take a moment to write also. I especially feel the need to respond to something that Dad said in his letter to me about the life I have "chosen for myself."

And, I am not writing this letter out of *criticism*, but mostly for myself, as I wrestle with all of this . . . so that I can read it on paper.

I have not *chosen* my sexual orientation. I did not choose to prefer men to women. Why would anyone chose possible persecution and ridicule? What I have done, quite simply . . . after about thirty-some years of doing what I was "supposed to do" . . . is *reclaim* my own body and soul.

I always felt strange. Different. And I never admitted even to myself what it was. Still today, I have a difficult time admitting who I am to myself. But I do feel better, more comfortable, more manly, more whole than I ever felt.

At the same time, while I have accepted a man into my life and into my bed, I would never choose this "lifestyle." I am only *accepting* what God has given me. And I am trying to understand and deal with "*why I am here.*"

I have decided that I am on this earth (this time) to help people understand about how they feel, and to communicate what I can about what it means to be human. I now have a unique perspective of men and women. And I am doing, performing, acting out, being assertive . . . as well as the feminine side—receptive, passive, creative. We all have both. Sex is not the issue.

With this in mind, I am going ahead with my final training toward my license as a psychotherapist. I'm on the right path for me.

My relationship with Dan is great. Different from anything I ever had. Something I longed for without knowing why I felt so lonely. Different than my marriage.

We are both very independent. He does not worship me. He does not desperately need me. He only wants and loves me. I need to learn all about quiet love. And about loving myself.

Thank you both for being there.

There is a gay man in one of my therapy groups whose parents told him that they wished he had died in Viet Nam, rather than being who he is. They didn't talk to him for seven years. Can you believe it?

Take care, Love,

Howard

CHAPTER FOURTEEN

Mark's Choice

For many years, during the hours my sons were in school, I worked part-time, at a job just 10 minutes from home. I arrived home, after school and work, at the same time Mark and Paul did.

I continued working, full-time, once Mark went off to college. By then, Paul was living at home, but teaching music at an adjacent community. He wanted *practical experience* before going back to college for his master's and doctorate degrees. He had earned a scholarship from the Eastman School of Music in Rochester, New York.

My work was not demanding. I got along just fine with my coworkers and my employer. And the extra money I earned made a difference in our family budget.

I've always hated to be idle! I've never been one to be bored with my own company! I thrive on action!

Mark often teased my about my *energy*. He would say such things as, "Mom! Where do you get such energy? You keep the house clean, do the laundry for all of us, go to work, come home, make dinner, then do all the marketing as well. You are *perpetual motion!* How do you do it?"

I could only tell him, "Son, I don't know. I guess it's my metabolism. This is me! Your Mom! But, if you and Paul didn't help with the dishes and your chores around the house, I wouldn't have the time or the energy to go to the market for shopping. You guys wouldn't have anything to eat."

We would have our chuckles and giggles over these subjects, then I would yell at him, "Go do your homework! Get off the phone, for a change!" He would go back to his work and I would continue with mine. I think now that both of us were unaware at the time that Mark had my perpetual-motion/constant-action characteristic.

His peers, friends, associates and others who knew him told me they had never known anyone who "moved like the wind," as Mark did. I understood him though! And he survived "the action."

When Bernie and I sold our home in Maplewood and moved to the apartment in Clark, I kept my job. Traveling to and from home and office was only 10 minutes each way before we moved. But, from Clark, it was 45 minutes one way. After a year of this routine, Bernie suggested, "Syl, you've been on the job for years. The kids are on their own now, and you've 'paid your dues,' so why don't you think about quitting and devoting more time to *yourself?*

"Your salary certainly comes in handy, but we can manage without it. Also, and maybe I'm being selfish, but I want to come home and find you rested, relaxed, and sitting on the terrace, reading a book while you wait for me to come home and give you a hug!"

I asked him, "What the heck will I do with myself, Bernie? You know I'm not one to go to luncheons with the women, nor spend my day dashing through department stores or sit through some discourse on cooking, baking or whatever!

"Bernie, you don't want me to sit around with other housewives and chatter about clothes do you? You know that's not my style!"

Bernie was insistent. "I understand all that. But what about the hobbies you've never had the chance to pursue? You love to read, and it would give you the chance to catch up on all the books you've never had time to read. And you like to paint. Why don't you join an art class? Sylvia, what's wrong with just doing nothing? You can have complete freedom to come and go at your own leisure!"

I resigned my job at the beginning of 1975 and enrolled in an art class which was conducted in our neighborhood one day a week. I also joined a health spa, where I went three days a week to enjoy gym, swimming, exercise and other activities. I even learned "belly dancing!" What a catastrophe!

For years before I quit the full-time work force, I belonged to various charitable organizations as a dues-paying, donor-but-non-active member. After "retirement," I found more time to be an active member, especially in the Organization for Rehabilitation Through Training (ORT).

Previously, in 1972, Bernie and I had visited Israel and enjoyed a tour there of ORT's rehabilitation center. We learned about the work they do around the world, in all nations. I was so impressed and touched that I joined ORT as soon as we came back home.

After leaving the full-time office routine, I volunteered to solicit donations of paintings for ORT's annual art shows.

I also did much reading, attended our son, Paul's, concerts, and listened to music. Often, I listened to audio tapes of Paul's beautiful music. My need to serve other humans was also fulfilled by my work for other charities.

With the nightmares of the summer of 1977 behind us, our lives took on new meaning. The special bond of love and closeness which our family has always shared became deeper and stronger. A new day dawned.

When fall arrived, in 1977, as the leaves were full of beautiful colors, I awoke early every morning with eagerness to face the day. I walked three miles daily, at daybreak, and savored the clean, clear, invigorating, healthy air.

When I was asked, "Why do you get up so early?" I joked, "I love to catch the good air before its all used up!"

I firmly believe morning exercise gives me the needed energy to face the day and the physical and mental strength to handle, logically, any problem which presents itself.

I missed this ritual while going through the trauma of the preceding months, even though I often felt the need to continue my walks. It would be a welcome stimulant, but I was physically and mentally fatigued from the lack of sleep, depression, stress and strain.

With the medicine the doctor gave Bernie, his blood pressure was under control and he was getting back to himself, emotionally and physically. He was completely involved in his work, back to being a "workaholic."

I looked forward to his coming home in the evening, and we would have dinner together, no matter what time—8:00, 9:00 or even 10:00. We talked out our day, and laughed about anything that had struck him funny during the coarse of his work. Bernie has an ability to apply humor to almost any situation, and his sense of humor once again was at the peak.

I would relate my activities, and we'd talk about Mark, Paul, and our daughter-in-law. We might watch a bit of television or read the newspapers. Sometimes we'd fall asleep during the 11 o'clock news.

We learned to accept what we cannot change! We found we didn't need to worry about things we can't do anything about.

We were so happy that once again we were "*with it!*" Our social life once more was back on the beam, and we didn't forget that humor is our best friend and temper our worst enemy.

Paul and his wife were doing fine; and Paul was advancing at the university, where he was composing and conducting such beautiful music.

Mark, at that time, was progressing wonderfully, happily working to complete his apprenticeship in public relations. He was acquiring his own clients and building himself a fine reputation. At the time, he was living in Greenwich Village, on Waverly Place, just opposite Washington Square.

Quite often he would invite us to spend a Sunday with him. "Have brunch in my apartment," he would say. "Afterward, we'll hit the action in the village."

He would also joke, "I know you two are early-birds, so don't get here too early! Give me a chance to sleep a little later. Make it about 10 o'clock."

162

We would get there early anyway, but to grab a parking space in front of his place, where we could leave the car for hours. Then, we'd walk around the village, killing time by window shopping, before the stores opened. The beautiful and varied items we would see in so many stores took us back to earlier years, when we took car trips to different places.

Years earlier, on a clear, brisk autumn Sunday morning, we packed lunch, piled the four of us, Bernie, Paul, Mark and me, in the car, and drove to an antique area in nearby Connecticut. The boys took games, books, whatever they wanted to occupy themselves, and a camera to take pictures of the beautiful countryside. Mother Nature was at her best that fall, and it was a beautiful sight to behold. It was a medley of colors: rust, yellow, orange and green, against a gorgeous blue sky!

It was not unusual for us to stop off at many shops on a day trip like that day. Six hours in the car was standard for three hours of shopping. And our appreciation for antiques rubbed off on Mark and Paul.

Bernie and I would remember those things as we walked in Greenwich Village, early in the morning. I would always buy something special from a gourmet bakery to add to our brunch. There would be fancy cookies, or other delectables we didn't find in our Jersey bakeries. We sometimes just sat in the park, munching cookies and people watching.

After mid-morning brunch with Mark, the three of us would browse through art galleries, antique shops and jewelry displays. We'd walk up one street and down another, sampling epicurean delights. Finally, exhausted, but happy and contented to be together, Bernie and I would leave for home, hoping to avoid late day traffic.

On some of our visits, Mark invited a friend or friends to join us. Debbie, Phil, Cathy, Cal. Male, female, gay, straight. Mark's friends were young, wonderful, friendly, sincere and interesting.

There was a special, deep bond between Debbie and Mark.

They had met in Boston while he was still at Emerson College. She had graduated from Emerson a few years earlier and was involved in theater in Boston. Debbie moved to New

York City and their bond became stronger and stronger. The love, devotion, respect and sincerity they shared was boundless.

We always had a grand time when we visited Mark and his friends. We looked forward to next time. And, sometimes he and his friends would come to visit us in Jersey, which also delighted us.

At that stage of Mark's life, he had not met the person with whom he felt he wanted to share a live-in arrangement and a commitment.

Another thing we shared with Mark and many of his friends was a fascination for the world of theater. Once Mark completed his apprenticeship, he was in a prestigious position with a prominent agency; and he specialized in the world of theater. Between the agency and his clients, Mark had a fine following.

He made it a point to invite Bernie and me to many broadway shows, and we often went backstage afterwards.

In June 1981, Mark was the press representative for the American Theater Wing's 35th Annual Antoinette Perry Awards ("Tony" Awards). We were invited to attend that momentous affair.

Bernie and I were in our glory and so very proud of our son. As busy as he was, running around supervising the even flow of the program, he found time to check with us during the evening, and make sure all was well. He introduced us to all the celebrities.

As a youngster, I loved movies and theater. I was a walking encyclopedia who knew everything about every movie and theater. I still have my scrapbook which I started when I was 12 or 13 years old. I have, for example, newspaper (now yellowing) and picture stories of Jean Harlow's life and death.

When I was just out of high school, I worked in a law office in downtown Newark, New Jersey. Every Saturday (that was in the early 1940s), we were open until noon. After work, two girlfriends and I would take the train out of nearby Pennsylvania Station into Manhattan.

After lunch, we would attend the matinee performance of the latest broadway show. We always sat first or second row center. This enjoyable Saturday afternoon procedure continued for many years. We saw many memorable performances.

Years later, when Mark and Paul were old enough to appreciate the theater, I would often take them to the Saturday matinee.

In 1964, Carol Burnett appeared on Broadway in *Fade Out—Fade In*. Bernie took the afternoon off and the four of us went to see the show. Afterward, Mark insisted that we wait at the stage door to meet Carol Burnett and get her autograph. It seemed we waited for hours, but we got her autograph.

I've often wondered if my love for the performing arts was inherited by Mark. Did this affect his choice of professions and his interest in theater?

During the summers, Mark and his friends rented a cottage at Fire Island. Getting away from the office for a long weekend was therapeutic for him. He loved the beautiful nature scene, the serenity of walking along the water's edge, sitting on the beach, watching the movement of the clear blue water and the foamy breakers crashing on the sand. Above him, the blue sky carried a few puffy clouds, and there would be a slight, soothing, gentle breeze. The sun was pleasant and warm, and birds soared up and down the beach. It was peaceful relaxation for mind and body.

During the summer of 1981, Mark met Edmund Wojcik, who was to become Mark's dear friend, devoted companion and lover in marriage.

Bernie and I first met Edmund the following November. Mark invited him to meet us at Mark's apartment before we left Jersey to spend the winter in Florida. In February, Mark telephoned us in Florida to let us know Edmund was moving in with him.

Edmund, Mark's Partner

Edmund Wojcik was born December 4, 1955 in Buffalo, New York. He was the youngest of five children, three girls and two boys.

Edmund is six feet, two inches tall, with fair complexion, straight brown hair (which he constantly brushes back), and sensitive hazel eyes.

He attended college in Pittsburgh, Pennsylvania. Initially undecided about his career, he ended up in the cosmetic and hair styling profession. He traveled the country as the personal cosmetician and hair stylist for Judy Collins.

Mark told us about his first meeting Edmund: "I was awakened about 6:30 on a Sunday morning by a cool breeze blowing through the open window along side my bed. As I sleepily rubbed my eyes, the clear, bright, unclouded blue sky came into focus.

I inhaled deeply, filling my lungs with the clean, fresh morning air. I exhaled to release the damaging chemicals in my body. I did it several times.

I could feel the energy surging through me while lying on the bed, listening to the surf splashing against the beach. The energy of the earth was flowing up through all parts of my body, and gently out through the top of my head.

I also felt the energy of the cosmos flowing in from the top of my head, circulating pleasantly in my body. What a sense of well being! The quiet peacefulness, the soothing, relaxing effect on my mind, the serenity. It sure felt good to be alive!

I thought about the contrast of Fire Island from the noisy, dirty, misty, polluted hustle and bustle of New York City. I laughed and thought to myself, 'Mom sure knows what she's doing when she gets up so early in the morning to breathe in the good, clean air before it's all used up. Yep!'

I jumped out of bed and put on a pair of swim trunks while my six male roommates still slept. We had rented the place together, and used it on alternate weekends.

166

On my way out, I took some money from my wallet to buy a *New York Times*. I also grabbed a dry towel to take with me, thinking I might take an early morning swim after my brisk walk.

Not far down the beach, I was surprised to see someone else out so early. Most everyone slept late on Sunday mornings, after having hectic Saturday nights to let off steam and release frustrations of the work week.

This tall, lanky guy was lying on his back, his head propped up high against a thick, folded beach towel. He never even stirred as I whizzed by. He was wearing dark glasses.

I bought my newspaper, had a cup of coffee and read for a bit before I started back. I walked casually. You don't jog or run with the heavy Sunday issue of the *New York Times*.

I saw him again as I walked back. This time, he was sitting along the shore line, with water rolling up all around him.

On impulse, I walked over to him and said, "Hi!" Are you catching the good morning air before it's all used up?"

He looked up at me as though I was out of my mind.

I laughed and explained, "My mother tells me it's the best time of day."

He stood up and said, "You're mother's right!"

I introduced myself. "I'm Mark Goldstaub, a publicist for the theater. And a good one," I added jokingly. "When I went by here an hour ago, you looked as though you were asleep."

He shook my hand as he said, "I'm Edmund Wojcik. No, I wasn't sleeping. I was comfortably relaxed, feeling somewhat a part of nature. The water was so calm and peaceful, it suspended all the problems and responsibilities for a while. I really enjoy the beauty, the sky, the birds. Mother Nature is a miracle.

As Mark and Edmund talked, Edmund explained that he was a cosmetologist and hair stylist. "I've been on the road with Judy Collins, and at the present time, I'm on hiatus for some R and R.

Mark agreed with Edmund's appreciation of Nature, and also wondered about their meeting.

Mark commented, "I wonder what the consequence will be of us meeting out here. In a few seconds, we find we have things in common. I often travel with my clients too."

They talked a while longer, and Mark said he felt they were destined to meet. He suggested, "Edmund, why don't you walk to my house—it's just a short distance from here— and I'll drop off the paper. Then we'll come back and sit by the water's edge and just talk. Maybe even take a swim together. I'll even invite you for breakfast. What do you say?"

Edmund responded, "Sounds good to me."

As they walked to the house, Mark asked, "Edmund, why haven't I seen you around here before?"

"As I said, I've been on the road a lot. I guess we just missed each other on weekends. Do you live in the city? My place is on the East Side."

Mark explained, "My apartment is on West 48th Street, between Eight Avenue and Ninth Avenue. Not the greatest neighborhood, but it's close to my office. 1501 Broadway. It's very convenient, especially when I work late at the office, then have to rush home, change clothes, grab a snack and be at the theater for an early night performance. And it beats waiting for a cab or riding the lousy subway!"

As Mark told Bernie and me later, "Well, that's how I met Edmund. Call it instinct or what, I just knew it was right for me."

EPILOGUE

There are so many things we human beings cannot understand, and we do not make any attempt to understand. When
adversity strikes, we question, "Why?" This encompasses all
individuals alike.

When we lost our beloved son, my world no longer seemed
to exist. I was very willing to withdraw myself and let life pass
me by. I felt my dreams and my future had been destroyed.

My husband, Bernie, would sit and talk with me for days
on end. "I too have lost a special son," he would remind me. "But
we still have our other special son, Paul. He's also a fine young
man and we'll always be proud of him too. We three still have
each other."

Bernie often repeated those words to me, ever since he
had first said them to me the night he found me on the floor of
the bedroom, crying.

I know now Bernie is right. I know this is what Mark wants
us to do. It had once been told to me that each of us is born with
inner wisdom, and inner strength to survive in our lifetime,
which is often filled with many trials and tribulations.

With age comes more wisdom, and this wisdom gives us the
courage to take charge of our lives. It provides the means to
take the necessary first positive step and to make a decisive step
that leads to action.

> God grant me the serenity to accept the things I cannot
> change, the courage to changes the things I can, and wisdom
> to know the difference.

I have been kept totally involved in replying to the hundreds of endearing cards, notes, and personally written letters of sympathy, admiration, respect and love that his friends felt for Mark. The daily flow of mail and tributes was endless.

I had no idea how widespread was my son's fine reputa-tion—in and out of the United States. I tried to keep up with the correspondence by answering every letter and card with my personal words. In between the many, many tears and emotional displays, and months later, I finally completed that sad chore.

I cannot deny the catastrophic loss in my life, but I must take each day, one day at a time. I know that I am capable of helping others cope with the loss of a loved one under the same circumstances. I am not surrendering to my grief.

There are periods when the enormity of my loss over-whelms me and I lapse into an emotional outburst. I lay down on my bed and let the tears flow. I fall asleep from complete exhaustion. When I awaken, I feel calmer.

In my search for the return of my plateau of acceptance of myself, through the group therapy programs I attend, I am re-establishing my self confidence, sense of self worth, self respect and self esteem. I have learned to avoid self deprecia-tion.

It is my goal now to carry the banner of humanity to other parents to enable them to open their hearts to their desperate children, many who are adults, and who need their parents' love.

I have developed the techniques of communicating to an audience of any size. I speak about the vital need for love and acceptance by parents, friends and relatives, and I tell about people with AIDS. I encourage people to develop an open, honest relationship. The response I receive is most rewarding and encouraging!

I am registered with various speaker's bureaus, but never in a million years did I think I would be able to stand up and project knowledge to an audience, and know by their attentiveness and questions that my message had reached them.

Mothers call me about their gay sons. "What to do?" Fathers call me about their lesbian daughters. "How to handle it?" Friends call me about their gay friends. All of them want me to help them.

Many have followed my suggestions to gather friends and relatives together, speak out and break *the silence about gays and lesbians with AIDS.* This openness and honesty has brought forth the knowledge that close friends and relatives are experiencing the same agonizing struggle, each keeping it from the other.

When we realize we are not alone in this struggle, we can share the emotional trauma and help them. Helping other families bond together with a cord of humanity and love has been good for me. I am happy to have reached them because my message comes from the heart. Being one who has lived it and is willing to share it with others helps them recognize their problem and relate to it.

I am making a difference for my son. I am his voice! I have become an outspoken advocate for the homosexual, the lesbian and the person with AIDS. I am the voice of so many people with AIDS who live their lives without family love.

I am a member and volunteer my services to many organizations for the advancement of acceptance and love, including, for example, P-FLAG (Parents and Friends of Lesbians and Gays). We open new windows of understanding. We are a volunteer organization of more than 200 chapters and contacts in the United States. Our chapters are beginning to grow in Australia, Canada and Europe.

P-FLAG provides support for families and friends of gay people, to help them understand and accept their gay loved ones. Every regional office in the federation has people who are ready to respond to the needs of families and friends of people with AIDS/ARC/HIV,

I am also an active volunteer for the Comprehensive Aids Program (CAP) of Palm Beach County, which provides case management, educational and volunteer services concerning HIV-spectrum diseases throughout Palm Beach County. For example, CAP helps with home nursing, mental health assessment, hospice care, social assistance, psychological support, medical and dental care, legal assistance, transportation, pediatric assistance, etc. This comprehensive AIDS program is a United Way Member Agency.

My volunteer services also encompass participation in the Legacy Foundation, a non-profit public charity organization dedicated to raising money for south Florida AIDS relief organizations. Musician Tom Danciu is its founder. He also founded *The Legacy Album*, produced by South Florida Musicians Unite for AIDS Relief. All proceeds from the album will go to AIDS relief and to help increase public awareness.

"An Ode To My Son Mark" is on the jacket of the album, and there is a spoken introduction by Dionne Warwick.

I am also a member of the American Foundation for AIDS Research, to which I donate whatever monies I am able to. I devote myself wholeheartedly to every facet of AIDS. I have the complete support of my husband, Bernie and son, Paul.

While going through the processes, I have to mentally and emotionally satisfy my deep inner compulsion to reach out—to be with my son, Mark—to touch him, kiss and hug him, talk with him and continue to love him. I often go back and remember the happy times, to escape from my tragic life. The energy of my loved ones becomes part of my energy. It flows in and out of me, through me. It sends spiritual vibrations and communication on a nonverbal level.

But, now I am fully on the path to help people to realize how much their son or daughter with AIDS needs them. They must have *Unconditional Love*. This is my mission, to help them find that!

* * * * *

Let us all stand together, mothers, fathers, brothers, *sisters, all peoples, mentally entwined all across the country and all around the world. Let us channel our hearts, our minds, our love, our energies, our hopes, our prayers toward the goal that in the not-too-distant future, science will find a cure for AIDS. No one knows what miracles could come to pass. Hope Springs Eternal!*

We received this letter from Debbie:

December 10, 1989

Dear Sylvia and Bernie,

As one year since Mark's death approaches within days, I finally was able, this morning, to verbalize to myself why, writing has not been possible up to this point. It is very simple. It has been too painful, and too private, to delve into my relationship with Mark, so I am hoping that the eulogy I wrote will give the reader a sense of my feelings for and about Mark.

Also, I have enclosed a photo of the quilt I made for Mark. The quilt took three months to make, utilizing every spare moment I had. Though I had never sewn anything before, I gave it all of my concentration, attention and energy whenever I wasn't at my job or sleeping. It helped me to stay grounded against the shock of Mark's death. It was a very therapeutic experience. Although the purpose in making the quilt was to honor Mark's life and death, the process gave back to me a focus, comfort, and a sense of being able to *do something* after grappling with the awful gnawing feeling of helplessness for two and one half years.

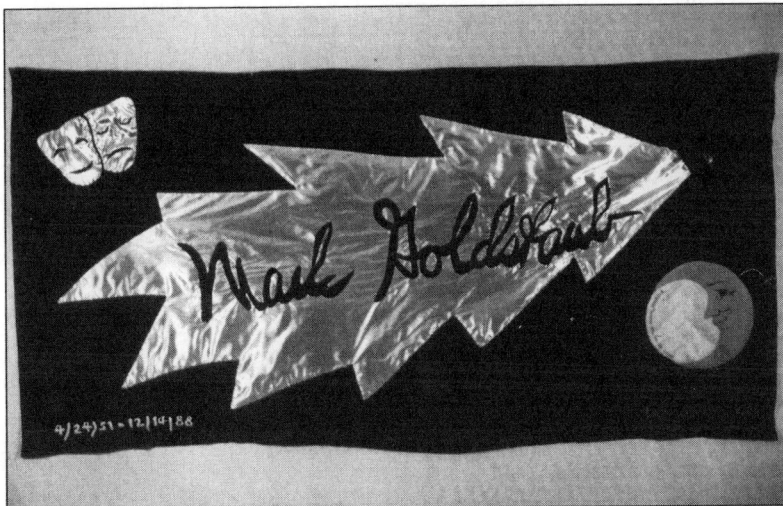

Debs' Quilt Was Made in Memory of Mark.

173

I was living in Virginia when Mark learned he had AIDS. I was already a volunteer with the local AIDS organization, Tidewater Aids Crisis Taskforce (TACT). During the last nine months of Mark's life, I participated in a bereavement group through TACT for persons who had lost loved ones to AIDS. I was told that I was suffering from "anticipatory grief," as Mark had died at that time. That certainly was the case and I was invited to join the group. I will always be grateful to TACT for providing that service, and always be grateful to my group "family," who shared their hearts, souls, tears, fears, laughter, hurts and hugs with me. They got me through. It filled my heart to present TACT with the quilt three months to the day after Mark's death at a "giving away ceremony," among members of the group. Though he never met them and never even heard about them, Mark was a very real person to a group of Virginians who sent him love every week.

A few words in explanation of the quilt: Mark's name is designed in his signature, the comedy and tragedy masks depict his love for and involvement in the arts, and mounted on the heart is a healing crystal I kept for him. The moon holds a special pull for me, so I have asked Mark to meet me there. "*Meet Me On the Moon, Markie!* The quilt is signed with the name he always called me, *DEBS.*

In closing, I want to say that I am very grateful for having had Mark in my life and feel very clear and clean about our relationship. I know we will meet again, and when we do, it will be with the same joy of instant recognition and love, only a thousandfold.

I am very pleased with what I wrote. It came straight from my heart. It is what I want to share with you. I look forward to reading your book and I am pleased to be a part of it.

Lots of love,
hugs and kisses,
Debs

174

APPENDIX

American Foundation for Aids Research (AMFAR)
1515 Broadway - Suite 3601
New York, NY 10036
Telephone: (212) 719-0033

American Foundation for Aids Research (AMFAR)
5900 Wilshire Boulevard - 2nd Floor
East Satellite
Los Angeles, CA 90036
Telephone: (213) 857-5900
AIDS Support Group (Terry Villaire)
Boca Raton Hospital Center
800 Meadows Road
Boca Raton, FL 33486
Telephone: (407) 395-7100

Comprehensive AIDS Program (CAP) of Palm
Beach County
2580 Metrocentre Boulevard - Suite 2
West Palm Beach, FL 33407
Telephone: (407) 687-3400

Compassionate Friends
ATTENTION: Jane DeBenedictis
470 S.E. 15th Avenue
Pompano Beach, FL 33060
Telephone: (305) 946-7825

Creative Visualization
Whatever Publishing Company, Inc.
P. O. Box 137
Mill Valley, CA 94941

Family Forum—Family Relations
ATTENTION: Helen Colton
1539 North Courtney Avenue
Los Angeles, CA 0\90046
Telephone: (213) 874-1410

Gay and Lesbian Alliance Against
Defamation (GLADD) L.A.
ATTENTION: Richard Jennings,
Executive Director
P. O. Box 931763
Hollywood, CA 90093-1763
Telephone: (213) 931-9429

GOD'S LOVE WE DELIVER, INC.
P. O. Box 1776 Old Chelsea Station
New York, NY 10113
Telephone: (212) 874-1193

Jewish Family Service
(A Division of South Palm Beach County
    Jewish Federation)
213000 Ruth and Baron Coleman Boulevard
Boca Raton, FL 33428
Telephone: (407) 852-3333

The LEGACY Foundation
ATTENTION: Tom Danciu
1329 S.E. Second Avenue
Deerfield Beach, FL 33441
Telephone: (305) 421-2384

Louise Hay
Hay House, Inc.
1154 East Dominguez Street
P. O. Box 27605
Carson City, CA 90749-6204
Telephone: (213) 395-7445
FAX: (213) 605-5313

Parents and Friends of Lesbians and Gays (P-FLAG)
P. O. Box 27605
Washington, DC 20038
Telephone: (202) 638-4200

Project Inform
347 Delores Street
Suite 301
San Francisco, CA 94110
Telephone: 1-(800)-822-7422 Toll Free

Recovery, Inc.
802 North Dearborn Street
Chicago, IL 60610

ABOUT THE AUTHOR

Sylvia Goldstaub was born in Newark, New Jersey. She met her husband, Bernard, while she was employed as a private secretary to a well-know workman's compensation attorney in downtown Newark.

Sylvia and Bernie were married in June 1945, and they raised two sons, Paul and Mark, while they lived most of their married life in Maplewood, New Jersey. Paul, the older son, is now Professor of Music and a noted composer and conductor at Ithaca College in upstate New York. Their younger son, Mark, who was President of Mark Goldstaub Public Relations for the theater, died of AIDS on December 14, 1988, at the age of 37.

Sylvia worked for the New Jersey Television Channel 13, in Trenton, New Jersey, as a television auction coordinator, and for many years, she was a volunteer publicist for various charity organizations, collecting works for their art auctions. Sylvia is also a portrait artist.

The Goldstaub family moved to Delray Beach, Florida, in November 1981.

After the death of their son, Mark, Sylvia and Bernie became very active with various AIDS support groups. They became surrogate parents to people with AIDS whose parents had rejected them and left them alone to die indigent. Learning of these tragedies, Sylvia brought the *humanistic side of AIDS* to the attention of the public. She speaks of *bonding the family.* She calls attention to families who fell apart because of parent's rejection of their own flesh and blood—their homosexual and lesbian children—some of whom had AIDS and others who did not.

Sylvia presents her personal experience with her son's AIDS in this powerful book, *"Unconditional Love: Mom! Dad! Love Me Please!'* In addition to honoring Mark through this writing, Sylvia has become a national speaker on the subject. She is the voice of her son. And she is the voice of all people with AIDS.

She has received many endorsements through her lectures, and radio and television appearances.

She is an active member of Parents and Friends of Lesbians and Gays (P-FLAG). Sylvia helped form the West Palm Beach branch of that organization. P-FLAG is a volunteer organization of more than 200 chapters in the United States, including chapters in Russia. They provide support for families and friends of gay people to help them understand and accept their gay loved ones. She is also very active in the South Palm Beach Comprehensive Aids Program (CAP), a public help agency funded in part by the United Way. And she is an active member of the American Foundation for AIDS Research (AMFAR).

Her poem, *"Ode to My Son Mark,"* appears on the jacket of *"The Legacy Album,"*, by South Florida Musicians Unite For AIDS Relief.

PHOTOS OF MARK AND SYLVIA GOLDSTAUB
BY CATHY BLAIVAS, NEW YORK CITY

POSTSCRIPT

GOD IS LOVE AND LIGHT! In Him, there is no darkness, and if we live with God in our hearts, we shall never fall, for love is the greatest gift of all.

People of all faiths can learn more about love from the scriptures. The following are some of my favorite passages from the *Holy Bible:*

Romans 3:20, 22-25
Romans 10:9, 10, 13
Romans 12:2
Romans 2:1
Galatians 2 and 3
Galatians 5:22-23
Ephesians 4:1-32
Ephesians 6:10-19
I John 1:9
I John 3:9
Matthew 7
Mark 13

If you ever feel religion in today's modern world has turned you away, read and study these words. The message is easy to understand, and you will find your life will improve.

— Coleen Moore
Harbor City Publications

For additional copies visit your
local bookstore.

Or you may order directly from
the Publisher.

Sylvia Goldstaub
6515 Kensington Lane
Suite #404
Delray Beach, Florida 33446
(407) 498-8614

Please enclose $14.95 per book
+ $1.50 shipping & handling.

Check or Money Order only.